THE
GOOD
FATHER

THE
GOOD
FATHER

A REVELATION OF OUR HEAVENLY FATHER WHO LOVES US AND CARES FOR US.

JEFFREY E ELLIS

The Good Father
Copyright © 2019 by Jeffrey Ellis

Facebook: https://www.facebook.com/ForgivingGod
Website: http://www.jeffellis.us

1st Edition. 2019

ASIN: (Amazon Kindle) B08237FTH5
ISBN: (Amazon Print) 9781712656174   PAPERBACK
ISBN: (Ingram Spark) 978-1-7326096-3-1 PAPERBACK
ISBN: (Ingram Spark) 978-1-7326096-1-7 HARDCOVER

Book Layout: © 2019 Evolve Global Publishing

66 All creation expectantly waits for the sons of God to be revealed. 99

ROMANS 8:19

Acknowledgement

My wife, Ginger, has been my faithful partner through this journey. We have ministered together in rescue missions, prisons, and jails for 20 years. She willingly proofread my drafts for accuracy, content, and "flow," improving them at every turn.

Our dear friends, Bill and Kelli Napp, offered immensely helpful critique, insights, and encouragement. We bless them on their journey. Sons, David Ellis and David Schmidgall, provided keen insights and commentary at critical phases of this project. Our love and prayers for their continued successes are unceasing.

As for the Lord, He is the true "author and finisher of our faith" (see Hebrews 12:2). He is a generous and patient Father, dearer to me now than ever before. He is the source and inspiration for this book. The praise, glory, and credit are all His.

Table of Contents

Introduction

By the time I was 38, my life was in shambles.

When I "came to myself" (see Luke 15), I had been drunk for sixteen years and addicted for longer than that. I was divorced, broke, jobless, homeless, living 1,100 miles away from my children, and totally alone. I had ruined every relationship in my life. Every dream I had was broken. I was discouraged, depressed, and ashamed. I was a mess.

Then someone came into my life and told me that God loved me and had a plan for my life. I needed both of those. So, on a beach in Maine in the middle of February 1995, I knelt down and asked Jesus to forgive me of my sins and to be the Lord of my life. It didn't seem like a life-changing moment at the time. I didn't know exactly what to do next, so I opened an old Bible and read the page I had opened. Luke 18:18 said to leave everything behind and come and follow Jesus. So, I did. From that moment on, everything began to change.

Over the next year, the Lord delivered me from bondage to alcohol and smoking. He reunited me with my children, who all got saved, too. He provided me with places to live, jobs, opportunities, cars, money, and a church. Soon, he provided me with a beautiful, godly wife, Ginger, and a mission. He propelled both of us into prison ministry. We started at a local men's rescue mission and then went into a state prison facility for the next seven years. We have spent the last 20 years reaching the lost and discipling believers behind bars.

But even as I have grown in the faith, I have always felt like there was more. Reading Smith Wigglesworth, A. W. Tozer, Kenneth Hagin, and Bill Johnson provoked me to seek more of God. I was dissatisfied, feeling like I knew about Him but didn't really know Him personally. I wasn't satisfied with other people's stories. I wanted to know God myself. I wanted my own Damascus road story. So, I went looking for Him.

And I found Him.

I found Him in prison cells and county jails, amidst the broken lives of inmates. I found Him in the songs of praise of 40 orphans, gathered before school in the cold mountains of India. I found Him in a country church, in the lives of quiet, honest people struggling with life. I found Him in hotel rooms, on my knees, crying out to Him. I found Him in my own life. I found Him everywhere. Now, He is the father I always wished I had. He is always with me, guiding, comforting, teaching, and revealing more and more of Himself.

He is the ultimate good Father.

This book is my story of discovering God and, in the process, discovering myself as His son. My prayer is that He might use this to bless someone, to reveal Himself to sons and daughters, to win their hearts as their heavenly Father.

Father

Creator

God created everything. To be more precise, He created everything from nothing. He created time and space and three dimensions in which "we move and live and have our being."[1] There is nothing around us that was not created by Him, including us! He created the first human being, Adam, out of dirt and dust. And He has created every person since.

To say that God is real is funny. I mean, He created real. All that we can sense and see and think and understand is the work of His hands. Try as I might, I can't find the words to describe Him. His power is indescribable. His mind is unsearchable. And His love for us is unstoppable.

When we consider our future and destiny, it's all about Him. Our legacies become memory and dust pretty quickly. We come into this world with nothing, and we take nothing out. The only thing that matters for eternity is the answer to one question: "What did you do with Jesus?"

However, when it comes to His plans and designs, it's all about us. We are His deepest affection. He reveals Himself to us in a million ways, day and night. He creates the stars and calls them by name. He sings over us, speaks to us, encourages us, beckons us. If we haven't heard His voice yet, it's because we aren't listening. He talks to us continually. He shows Himself repeatedly.

God's desire is for us to know Him, to know that He loves us and is not angry with us. This is the God who is always good, in whom there is not even a shadow of evil.[2] With Him is the joy, peace, and freedom for which we hunger, now and forever.

Father is exceedingly abundant and generous. Everything He does is extravagant. He is faithful through every season. He never wavers in His grand, over-the-top affection for us. He goes to great lengths to win our hearts for Himself. He fights like a determined warrior to rescue us.

God is our peace in the midst of the storms. He is a blast of thunder to His enemies. He is our stillness in the early morning and calmness in the evening. He gives us everything we need for this life and the next. He sent His son to bear sickness and death so that we don't have to.[3] He has given us authority over the enemy, power over death, and victory over defeat.

It is not possible to exaggerate the goodness of God. His own testimony is that every good and perfect gift is given to us, by Him.[4] In Him, we have joy, peace, plenty, and love. He is the father we continually need: giving, caring, kind, protective, strong, selfless. He is kind, gracious, and protective beyond measure.

The love we feel came from Him in the first place. The breath in our lungs, the firing of the synapses in our brains, the cry of praise from our mouths and worship from deep within our souls all begin with Him. We love Him because He first loved us.[5]

The more I get to know God, the fewer words I find to describe Him. Until there are no words left at all… but to simply bow my head and fall silent, in witness of Him.

Our Heavenly Father

God is a good father. The very best.

He is intimately acquainted with each of us. He knew us even before we were born. Forming each of us in our mothers' wombs,[6] He designed us for a special purpose. Our abilities, gifts, and talents are testimonies of His grand design.

Today, we know Him as our loving father, but back in the early days, the Jewish people didn't know Him that way. They knew Jehovah as their provider, shepherd, healer, and other manifestations. But they didn't know Him as Dad, or Abba.[7] When Jesus came to earth and declared God as His Father and ours, He changed the world forever. What was blasphemy to the lawyers and priests became the great hope of mankind.

Some of the Old Testament names of God were:

Jehovah Jireh[8] – provider

Jehovah Shammah[9] – presence

Jehovah Shalom[10] – peace

Jehovah Tsidkenu[11] – righteousness

Jehovah Rophe[12] – healer

Jehovah Rohi[13] – shepherd

Jehovah Nissi[14] – banner

Notice that Jehovah Abba is not listed. It would take a major move of God, a stunning entrance into the world of a son, Jesus, to reveal that relationship.

When Jesus taught His disciples to pray saying, "Our Father,"[15] He revealed a relationship the world had never known. Jesus revealed God as a father. With this new relationship, Jesus ushered in a new covenant. Notice that Jesus said, *Our* Father, not *My* Father. He had every right to declare God as His Father, but He didn't. When He used the word "our," he included His followers in that relationship, too. He included you and me.

Seeking Him

What is the "secret" to knowing Father? It lies in seeking him. Deuteronomy 4:29 says that we shall find God when we seek Him with all our heart and soul." "Seek Him while He can still be found."[16] "Seek first the Kingdom of God and His righteousness."[17] Paul tells us that He is a "rewarder of those who diligently seek Him."[18] Seek Him early, before everything else. This is the beginning of knowing Him. We can know about Him through his Word. We come to know Him by seeking his face.

There is no greater love, more charming personality, more profound presence than Father's. On this, I have staked my life. I am in His hands where there is no risk, no downside. He is well able to perform all that he has in mind for me.[19]

Knowing Him

It is possible for us to know God. And more than possible. It is His will for us to know Him deeply and intimately. Jesus came to earth to reveal Him as our Father. He paid the ultimate price so that we might enter into a close, personal, loving relationship with the one who loves us more than life. God has a warm personality, sense of humor, and tenderheartedness toward His sons and daughters. He is patient, long-suffering, and graceful. As I get to know Him, I realize more and more how little I really know Him. The greatness of Him swallows up the smallness of me. And, all the while, He beckons me to know him deeper still.

We know that, one day, we will see our Father face to face (See 1 Corinthians 13:12). In the meantime…

We do know that God is powerful.

He is endlessly imaginative.

He is faithful, kind, loving, and attentive.

He cares about everything in our lives.

He is a good Father.

Spirit to Spirit

God is spirit.[20] As we seek Him, He reveals more and more of Himself to us. However, we do not experience Him *primarily* through our natural senses (sight, sound, touch, etc.) but through our spiritual senses, which requires that we are spiritually alive.

We are three-part beings: body, soul, and spirit.[21] When we accept Jesus as our savior and ask Him to forgive us our sins, we are saved; we are "born again."[22] Being born again refers to our spiritual selves being reborn, not our physical selves. The Holy Spirit comes and lives in us and, suddenly, our spirits are reborn.[23]

Once our spirits are brought to life, we become vibrant, sensitive, and aware of the spiritual realm. For the most part, Father communicates with us through our spirit. While He is fully capable of appearing in the natural realm or speaking aloud or anything He chooses to do, He primarily communicates with our spirits.

As we become accustomed to being spiritually alive, we develop a growing awareness of His presence. We can tell when He is in the room. This is called "quickening." When the presence of the Holy Spirit is strong in me, He feels like electrified, warm honey.

When we are saved, the Holy Spirit lives in us.[24] Subsequently, when we are filled to overflowing with the Spirit, He is revealed by boldness and speaking in tongues.[25] This experience is called the baptism of the Holy Spirit and is described in Acts (see Chapter 2) and repeatedly throughout the New Testament.[26] This is the fulfillment of the promise Jesus made when He said, "You will be endued with power from on high."[27] While all believers receive the Holy Spirit when they are born again, there is even more spiritual presence available. We can be filled to overflowing like the early disciples and apostles were. This experience is available for the asking (see Luke 1:15, Luke 4:1, Acts 2:4, Acts 4:8, Acts 4:31, Acts 7:55, Acts 13:9, Acts 13:52). Being filled with the Holy Spirit makes us more acutely aware of the presence of God and quickens us to hear His voice.

God Himself provides us with everything we need for a close, loving relationship with Him. He gives us a private prayer language to speak with Him. He ignites our hearts to worship. He gives us boldness in declaring who He is and what He has done. He gives us a testimony laden with power to set us free and to inspire others. He is alive and living within us and accomplishing everything He has set out to perform in heaven and earth. He still is everything He ever was. All the gifts of the Spirit are as available today as they ever were. The Lord has not changed.[28]

I know this description of Father mystifies some. Scientists and doctors and intellectuals are frustrated that God doesn't show Himself on command. He does not constrain Himself to the laws of science and nature. The laboratory cannot contain Him. He does not submit to the scientific method. He cannot be studied in test tubes and clinical trials. He must be experienced on His terms, not ours. He exists outside the laws of nature. He exists outside of time. He lives in a realm of His own making and invites us to share it with Him.

Many believers feel that God is too removed, too greatly engaged with the affairs of the universe to care about them. While they can believe that God is in control of the major events of mankind, He must be too busy with the affairs of the universe to be concerned with the small issues of their lives.

The God of the universe cares about the things we care about, large and small. In a grand way, He changed our destinies by sending His son, Jesus, to die in our place. In small ways, He concerns Himself with every detail of our lives.

In 1996, I was a baby Christian at the early stages of God's reconstruction plan for my life. I was broke. One night as I was driving to church near Chicago, I stopped at the toll booth to pay the 40-cent toll. To this day, I remember feeling the smooth bottom of the change compartment in the car as I pulled out the coins. I thought to myself, "I need to ask someone at church for 40 cents to get home." After the service, I headed home. I arrived at the tollbooth and suddenly remembered that I had no money. Frantically, I patted down my pockets, checked my wallet, and opened the change compartment, even though I knew it was bare. To my amazement, my fingertips felt coins! Sure enough, a quarter, dime, and nickel. This was the first, and smallest, of many miracles that the Father would delight in doing for me. He cares about the small things in our lives, even 40-cent miracles!

While this miracle might seem silly and small to some people, it was a big deal to me. In that moment, I knew that God was real. And I knew that He cared about me. He knew what I needed and delivered a miracle. Then it dawned on me; if He cared about small things, surely, He cared about big things. If He would do a creative miracle with small change, I knew I could call on Him for the big stuff: healing, deliverance from my addictions, salvation for my children, and more. Furthermore, He was interested in the details of my life. He concerned Himself with the things that concerned me. To this day, 23 years later, I thank the Lord, out loud, each time I go through a toll booth.

He still amazes me.

The Choice

Sooner or later, everyone faces a dilemma of faith. Will we accept God as He is or insist that he conform to our understanding? Are we willing to believe without seeing? Are we willing to see the invisible, cling to the untouchable, experience the one who exists outside of our experience? Can we really know such a father? Can we really love such a father?

The answer is yes, yes, yes!

There is nothing greater than knowing God. He is the wonder in every discovery. He is the solution to every problem. He is the healing to every disease, life to every deadness, the joy to every despair. He is the hope our hearts long for. I pray that the restless, pensive cry of this generation turns to Him for fulfillment. We are among a lost generation of orphans[29] longing for a father's love.

The ultimate irony is that He is always available to everyone on earth. He desires to be a father to us all. And that loving relationship is within the grasp of each of us. But the Lord does not force Himself on anyone. He is a perfect gentleman. The offer is extended to all but must be accepted. He has made it exceedingly simple; we must be reconciled to him, the rags of orphanhood removed. How? Here is a salvation prayer that gets that done:

"Jesus, please forgive me of my sins and come into my life as Lord and savior."[30]

More

Praying that prayer from the heart brings salvation (see Romans 10). That's the beginning. And for everyone with a seeking heart, there is much, much more. All the books ever written, in every library in the world, cannot contain the deeds and wonders of God or the plans He has for each of us. Each child experiences Him for themselves, exquisitely, as Father shows Himself to each of us. Each one of us is His favorite (even though He doesn't play favorites). I know that is a contradiction. Welcome to paradox. Welcome to the Kingdom of God.

The Cost

So, what does this experience of "knowing God" cost? Everything. It costs everything. To fully enter into this relationship, we must be willing to be dead to ourselves and alive to God.[31] Then, having made the sacrifice, we don't get to crawl off the altar and resume our old ways. Where, then, is the upside? We get all of Him. I'll make that trade. All the junk in my life in exchange for Him? Done.

Love instead of hatred, jealousy, and selfishness? Turmoil for peace? Fear for faith? Provision for poverty? Healing for sickness? Life for death? Seriously? Done, done, a thousand times done.

ENDNOTES
Chapter One

1. "for in Him we live and move and have our being, as also some of your own poets have said, 'For we are also His offspring.'" Acts 17:28 NKJV
2. "Every good gift and every perfect gift is from above, and comes down from the Father of lights, with whom there is no variation or shadow of turning." James 1:17 NKJV
3. "who Himself bore our sins in His own body on the tree, that we, having died to sins, might live for righteousness—by whose stripes you were healed." I Peter 2:24 NKJV
4. "Every good gift and every perfect gift is from above, and comes down from the Father of lights, with whom there is no variation or shadow of turning." James 1:17 NKJV
5. "We love Him because He first loved us." 1 John 4:19 NKJV
6. "For You formed my inward parts; You covered me in my mother's womb. I will praise You, for I am fearfully and wonderfully made; Marvelous are Your works, And that my soul knows very well." Psalms 139:13–14 NKJV
7. "And Abraham called the name of the place, The-LORD-Will-Provide; as it is said to this day, "In the Mount of the LORD it shall be provided." Genesis 22:14 NKJV
8. "And Abraham called the name of the place, The-LORD-Will-Provide; as it is said to this day, "In the Mount of the LORD it shall be provided."" Genesis 22:14 NKJV
9. "All the way around shall be eighteen thousand cubits; and the name of the city from that day shall be: THE LORD IS THERE." Ezekiel 48:35 NKJV
10. "So Gideon built an altar there to the LORD, and called it The-LORD-Is-Peace. To this day it is still in Ophrah of the Abiezrites." Judges 6:24 NKJV
11. "In His days Judah will be saved, And Israel will dwell safely; Now this is His name by which He will be called: THE LORD OUR RIGHTEOUSNESS." Jeremiah 23:6 NKJV
12. "and said, "If you diligently heed the voice of the LORD your God and do what is right in His sight, give ear to His commandments and keep all His statutes, I will put none of the diseases on you which I have brought on the Egyptians. For I am the LORD who heals you." Exodus 15:26 NKJV
13. "The LORD is my shepherd; I shall not want." Psalms 23:1 NKJV

14. "And Moses built an altar and called its name, The-LORD -Is-My-Banner." Exodus 17:15 NKJV
15. "In this manner, therefore, pray: Our Father in heaven, Hallowed be Your name." Matthew 6:9 NKJV
16. "Seek the LORD while He may be found, Call upon Him while He is near." Isaiah 55:6 NKJV
17. "But seek first the kingdom of God and His righteousness, and all these things shall be added to you." Matthew 6:33 NKJV
18. "But without faith it is impossible to please Him, for he who comes to God must believe that He is, and that He is a rewarder of those who diligently seek Him." Hebrews 11:6 NKJV
19. "But without faith it is impossible to please Him, for he who comes to God must believe that He is, and that He is a rewarder of those who diligently seek Him." Hebrews 11:6 NKJV
20. "God is Spirit, and those who worship Him must worship in spirit and truth." John 4:24 NKJV
21. "Now may the God of peace Himself sanctify you completely; and may your whole spirit, soul, and body be preserved blameless at the coming of our Lord Jesus Christ." 1 Thessalonians 5:23 NKJV
22. "That good thing which was committed to you, keep by the Holy Spirit who dwells in us." 2 Timothy 1:14 NKJV
23. "Or do you not know that your body is the temple of the Holy Spirit who is in you, whom you have from God, and you are not your own?" I Corinthians 6:19 NKJV
24. Ibid.
25. "But now, brethren, if I come to you speaking with tongues, what shall I profit you unless I speak to you either by revelation, by knowledge, by prophesying, or by teaching?" I Corinthians 14:6 NKJV
26. "Then Peter said to them, 'Repent, and let every one of you be baptized in the name of Jesus Christ for the remission of sins; and you shall receive the gift of the Holy Spirit'."Acts 2:38 NKJV; "And as I began to speak, the Holy Spirit fell upon them, as upon us at the beginning. Then I remembered the word of the Lord, how He said, 'John indeed baptized with water, but you shall be baptized with the Holy Spirit.'" Acts 11:15–16 NKJV; "And when they had prayed, the place where they were assembled together was shaken; and they were all filled with the Holy Spirit, and they spoke the word of God with boldness." Acts 4:31 NKJV; "But he, being full of the Holy Spirit, gazed into heaven and saw the glory of God, and Jesus standing at the right hand of God." Acts 7:55 NKJV; "And those of the circumcision who believed were astonished, as many as came with Peter, because the gift of the Holy Spirit had been poured out on the Gentiles also." Acts 10:45 NKJV

27. "Behold, I send the Promise of My Father upon you; but tarry in the city of Jerusalem until you are endued with power from on high.'" Luke 24:49 NKJV
28. "Jesus Christ is the same yesterday, today, and forever." Hebrews 13:8 NKJV
29. "I will not leave you orphans; I will come to you." John 14:18 NKJV
30. "So they said, 'Believe on the Lord Jesus Christ, and you will be saved, you and your household.'" Acts 16:31 NKJV
31. "Likewise you also, reckon yourselves to be dead indeed to sin, but alive to God in Christ Jesus our Lord." Romans 6:11 NKJV

Who Are We?

Orphans

Let's start at the beginning. Sin made us all orphans.[1]

While we are all *creations* of God, we are not all *children* of God. Although we bear the family resemblance, we are not adopted into the family until we make that decision for ourselves. Some will, and some won't.

There is a popular sentiment that says, "We are all God's children." The basis for this is that everyone is "made in the image of God."[2] God created Adam "in His image,"[3] and we have all descended from Adam, so we too bear resemblance to the Father.

I understand the allure of this argument, but it doesn't seem to agree with what God has said. It would be great if, simply by being born, we all were considered sons of God, but that doesn't appear to be what He said:

> "But as many as received Him, to them He gave the right to become children of God, to those who believe in His name."
> John 1:12 NKJV

> "For you are all sons of God through faith in Christ Jesus."
> Galatians 3:26 NKJV

Paul makes it clear in his letter to believers in Galatia that it was *their faith in Jesus* that made them sons of God,[4] not just being born into the world. If we were automatically children of God by birth, we wouldn't have to do anything else to attain it. But we do. We have to believe in Jesus. He taught that entering into relationship with God, becoming His child, required a spiritual birth, not a physical birth. Simply being born into the world is not what it takes to enter into the family of God.

> "Jesus answered, 'Most assuredly, I say to you, unless one is born of water and the Spirit, he cannot enter the kingdom of God. That which is born of the flesh is flesh, and that which is born of the Spirit is spirit. Do not marvel that I said to you, "You must be born again."'" John 3:5–7 NKJV

In fact, those who are born again are so different, those in the world do not even recognize them for who they really are: sons and daughters of God.

> "Behold, what manner of love the Father hath bestowed upon us, that we should be called the sons of God: therefore, the world knows us not, because it knew him not." 1 John 3:1 KJV

The hard lesson here is that we don't get to alter the standard to fit our culture or personal preferences. Truth stands alone, unmoved and unchanged by how we may feel about it.

Adoption

This is a reverse adoption. Father has already chosen us; He wants to adopt us, but we must accept *Him*. He gives *us* the choice to enter into that special relationship with Him; He does not force Himself on us. And love always gives us the right to choose. Love is always a choice.

How is this accomplished? Simple. God gives us the right to become His children when we believe and receive Jesus as our savior.[5] (Please note: the word "son" also means daughter). In that moment, we become His children. According to the original language, it is our birthright or privilege,[6] available to everyone. We are then considered family, sealed by the spirit of adoption.[7]

"For you did not receive the spirit of bondage again to fear, but you received the Spirit of adoption by whom we cry out, 'Abba, Father.'" Romans 8:15 NKJV

God's offer of adoption is available to everybody, but it has to be accepted, it has to be received to be accomplished. Adoption is a contractual agreement; both parties have to say "yes." For His part, God accepts everyone who will.[8] And some will, and some will not. Each of us must make that choice for herself or himself. The Passion Translation puts it this way:

"But you have received the 'Spirit of full acceptance,' enfolding you into the family of God. And you will never feel orphaned, for as he rises up within us, our spirits join him in saying the words of tender affection, 'Beloved Father!'" Romans 8:15 TPT

And this in Galatians:

"But when the fullness of the time had come, God sent forth His Son, born of a woman, born under the law, to redeem those who were under the law, that we might receive the adoption as sons. And because you are sons, God has sent forth the Spirit of His Son into your hearts, crying out, 'Abba, Father!' Therefore, you are no longer a slave but a son, and if a son, then an heir of God through Christ." Galatians 4:4–7 NKJV

Let's be clear. Adoption by Father is a gift. All we do is receive it; He does the rest. He forgives us, cleanses us of a lifetime of sin, gives us His righteousness, His holiness, and then hugs us till we gasp for air. As His children, we inherit all that He promises. We share in all His riches. Most of all, we have Him. We cannot earn this indescribable gift. He gives it to us because of His nature, not ours.

This point was driven home one day as I was returning a rental car at the airport. The Lord broke through my internal dialogue and spoke to me: "Jeffrey, I do not love you for *what you do or don't do. I love you for *who you are.*" Those words forever changed how I saw my Father.

He loves me because of our relationship, because I am His son. As a Father, I understand that. I don't love my children because of what they do or don't do. I love them because of who they *are*, my sons and daughters. Obviously, this doesn't give us license to sin. He calls us to a better life than that. But it does show us the way home.

Sometimes, we may feel we don't deserve His attention, love, or affection. Many believers feel unworthy. This is a trap that keeps us from entering into a deeper, stronger relationship with God. Unworthiness sounds like humility, but it's unbelief in disguise. It's simply not believing that what God says about us is true.

It is natural for us to feel unworthy of such a great and mighty Father and King. But we are not children of the natural; we are children of the supernatural. We are worthy of His affection and attention not because we say so, but because He says so. Look, in ourselves, we are not good enough, not righteous enough, not loving enough to deserve His love, grace, and mercy. He seems way beyond our reach. But God doesn't require that we reach Him; instead He reaches for us. When we say "Yes, Father," He does the rest. His arms are long and strong enough to get it done.

The fact is, there is too much at stake for us to have a lower (or higher) opinion of ourselves than He has. Our unsaved families and friends hang in the balance. Our friends and colleagues don't know him. Even if our own walk may be halting or uncertain, we cannot afford to think less of ourselves than He does!

Bill Johnson says it best: "I cannot afford to have a thought in my mind about me that is different than what He thinks about me."[9] We fool ourselves if we believe the lies of the enemy about us. His wicked voice whispers in our ears, "You aren't good enough, strong enough, smart enough, worthy enough, etc."

That is not the truth. In Him, we are worthy. In Him, we are complete. In Him, we are strong and smart and able to do everything! In Him, we are whole, sound, and healed with nothing broken and nothing lacking. In this way, we take our places as family. And when we do, a deep confidence and holy boldness rises up inside us until we can shout, "All things are possible![10] I can do all things because of Jesus!"[11]

When we believe Him and what He says about us, we grow in the Lord. When His Word is in conflict with what we see and hear and feel and we choose to believe Him, we take a step forward. We will be tested again and again; it is the nature of the world versus the Kingdom of God. So, when the critical diagnosis is received or the bad report is given, what will we believe? Will we believe that we are healed by the blood of Jesus? Will we seek him for our healing or panic? Will we accept or refuse the bad report? God's promises are always superior to what others say. Our spirit bears witness with His Spirit that we can trust him with great confidence.[12]

God always has the last word. The Father's promises are always superior to the laws of nature and man. Disease must flee before the healing indignation of Jesus. Poverty must crumble as His bountiful provision is delivered. Clouds of hopelessness and depression dissipate in the brightness of His shining. And every work of the enemy is destroyed in the power of His presence.

If He says that I am hidden in Christ,[13] then I am hidden. If He says all of my insecurities and failings and fears are swallowed up in the magnificence of Jesus, then they are. If the Father says He sees me like He sees Jesus, then He is correct. And if He has taken all of my sins and shortcomings on Himself, never more to be held against me, then I have a fresh start.[14] I am a new person.[15]

It is this very anthem of heaven that shouts to all creation, "God has given Him a name above every name. At the name of Jesus, every knee shall bow and tongue confess that Jesus Christ is Lord, to the glory of God the Father!"[16] Feelings of shame, regret, and unworthiness must bow the knee to the name of Jesus. Disease, loss, despair, sadness, and death bite the dust in the presence of the Lord Jesus.

It is this confidence that causes us to boldly face the future, secure in the knowledge of the Anointed One. The apostle John taught this saying: "Greater is he who is in you than he who is in the world."[17] And Paul wrote, "I can do all things through Christ which strengthens me."[18] All things.[19] Imagine, *all* things. Amazing truth.

This is the heritage for the children of the Lord: If God gave us Jesus, He gave us everything.[20] We can do all things through Jesus[21]. His greatness overshadows our smallness. God's view of us wins.

Sons and Daughters

There was a tradition in ancient Israel in which a father presented his son, around thirty years old, to the village. In front of the village elders, businessmen, and tradespeople, the father would announce, "This is my son. He acts in my authority. When you deal with him, you're dealing with me."[22] It was a coming-of-age ritual that announced to the world that his son had authority, responsibility, and privilege to act on the father's behalf, to act in his name.

This is beautifully and powerfully captured in Matthew 3:17 when Jesus was thirty years old and Father tore open the sky and announced to the world, "This is my beloved son in whom I am well pleased!" The Holy Spirit then descended on Jesus and remained with Him, anointing and empowering all of His words and deeds. Note that this affirmation was made *before* Jesus began His ministry, illustrating that He loves us for who we are *in Him*, not what we do *for Him*.

In a similar way, when we become sons of God, we become heirs and receive what Christ has obtained on our behalf. What does that mean for us? We are no longer beggars. We are sons and daughters of God. We have access to Him, to the throne of grace; our petitions are heard and acted upon. We have the right to use His name to stand against the enemy. We are covered in love and protected by the blood of Jesus. We are given authority to act in the name of Jesus, and the resources of heaven are assembled to stand with us. We have the power and authority to cast out sickness, discouragement, depression, and death. We have the power and authority to insist that the Word of God be accomplished in the world over every objection of the enemy. And much, much more.

The entire universe is standing on tiptoe, watching to see the full impact of our inheritance. To see the unveiling of God's sons and daughters.[23]

"But now, with eager expectation, all creation longs for freedom from its slavery to decay and to experience with us the wonderful freedom coming to God's children. To this day we are aware of the universal agony and groaning of creation, as if it were in the contractions of labor for childbirth.

And it's not just creation. We who have already experienced the first fruits of the Spirit also inwardly groan as we passionately long to experience our full status as God's sons and daughters—including our physical bodies being transformed. For this is the hope of our salvation." Romans 8:14–24 TPT

How do we know what to do, how to act, what to believe? Jesus is our example. And we are called to be like Him, act like Him, and love like Him. According to the Father, we are being transformed to be just like Him.

"We are being transfigured into his very image as we move from one brighter level of glory to another. And this glorious transfiguration comes from the Lord, who is the Spirit." 2 Corinthians 3:18 TPT

"For he knew all about us before we were born, and he destined us from the beginning to share the likeness of his Son. This means the Son is the oldest among a vast family of brothers and sisters who will become just like him." Romans 8:29 TPT

And 1 John 3:12 says that when we see Him, we will be like Him:

"Beloved, now we are children of God; and it has not yet been revealed what we shall be, but we know that when He is revealed, we shall be like Him, for we shall see Him as He is."

Consider this amazing fact, **"all that Jesus now is, so are we in this world."** 1 John 4:17 TPT

All that Jesus is, Lord of Lords and King of Kings, the Son of God, seated at the right hand of God, is ours today. Not "someday, when we get to glory" but right here, right now. Notice too, the Spirit is not referring to the Christ suffering on the cross. That is not our burden. He paid that price. His sacrifice was enough and more than enough to satisfy the judgement of our holy Father. No, the reference is to Jesus as He is now, in power and glory forever.

All that He has and all that He is is ours. Let me put it another way: We are who Jesus is today. Some will say, "Wait a minute. We are not the equal of Jesus." That is true. He came as a singular, perfect sacrifice for the world, and we are not asked to do that. The assignment we have been given is to serve the world with all that He obtained on our behalf.

We need to get this right. There is a danger here on both sides of the road. On one side is pride, that we consider ourselves more important than we are. We are still human, not glorified yet. In and of ourselves, we are dirt and dust, and we should not think of ourselves more than we ought.[24] Nevertheless, we are children of the King and endowed with His nature, authority, and power, according to what He has told us. We have what He has because He is giving it to us, not because we deserve it. So, we minister with a humble servant spirit. As Pastor Bill Johnson beautifully put it, "We rule with the heart of a servant and serve with the heart of a king."[25]

How does this change our lives, our prayers, our destiny? In a word, it changes everything. It changes how we pray, how we conduct ourselves, how we see our future; all of it changes. The Father receives us as sons. I am not talking about chasing money, although we must not be backwards and ashamed about finances. I am talking primarily about kingly resources of authority, power over the enemy, peace, righteousness, holiness, generosity, graciousness, and justice. Make no mistake, poverty is a curse and the Father has redeemed us from the power of the curse.[26]

As sons and daughters, we are healed, whole, saved, lifted up, filled up, dressed up, embraced, encouraged, victorious, highly favored, and greatly beloved. Our destiny knows no bounds, our future is secure, our legacy extends to the generations as our whole household is saved. We live in peace and battle in power. We have dignity and identity with the Anointed One who is above all in heaven and earth. Our past is forgotten, our present is overflowing, and our future is radiant with possibility. We walk in love, pray with confidence, and speak with wisdom. We are forgiving, gracious, generous, gentle, loving, and kind. We are kids of the King and heirs to the throne. What a legacy we have: riches beyond measure and love beyond our frailties and faults.

What, then, are we to do now? We are to obey the directives of the Father. We are to go into the world and declare the Kingdom of God.[27] We are to move in power, breaking every work of the enemy[28] and releasing the power of God among men and women. We are to do what Jesus told us to do in Matthew 10:7–8: "Preach, saying the Kingdom of Heaven is at hand. Heal the sick, cleanse the lepers, raise the dead, and cast out demons." Our assignment is to transform the world under the direction and power of God. We execute this assignment as servants, not tyrants.

What does that mean for us? We have access to the throne of grace, our petitions are heard and acted upon,[29] we have the right to use His name to stand against the enemy, and we are covered in love and protected by the blood of Jesus. We are given authority to act in the name of Jesus and the resources of heaven are assembled to stand with us. And much, much more.

I would like to point out a trap in front of us. We do not become sons and daughters for what we get out of the deal. Even as Father loves us for who we are, we also love Him for who He is, not for what He does for us. To do otherwise would reduce Him to a supernatural ATM machine and turn the relationship into manipulation and selfish consumerism. The desire of our hearts is to love Him because of who He is: our Father who is in heaven.

ENDNOTES
Chapter Two

1. "I will not leave you orphans; I will come to you." John 14:18 NKJV
2. "So God created man in His own image; in the image of God He created him; male and female He created them." Genesis 1:27 NKJV
3. Ibid.
4. "For you are all sons of God through faith in Christ Jesus." Galatians 3:26 NKJV
5. "But as many as received Him, to them He gave the right to become children of God, to those who believe in His name:" John 1:12 NKJV
6. Ibid.
7. "For you did not receive the spirit of bondage again to fear, but you received the Spirit of adoption by whom we cry out, "Abba, Father." Romans 8:15 NKJV
8. "For whoever desires to save his life will lose it, but whoever loses his life for My sake and the gospel's will save it." Mark 8:35 NKJV
9. Bill Johnson (2007). "Strengthen Yourself in the Lord: How to Release the Hidden Power of God in Your Life", p. 62, Destiny Image Publishers
10. "But Jesus looked at them and said to them, "With men this is impossible, but with God all things are possible." Matthew 19:26 NKJV; "Jesus said to him, "If you can believe, all things are possible to him who believes." Mark 9:23 NKJV
11. "I can do all things through Christ who strengthens me." Philippians 4:13 NKJV
12. "The Spirit Himself bears witness with our spirit that we are children of God," Romans 8:16 NKJV
13. "For you died, and your life is hidden with Christ in God." Colossians 3:3 NKJV
14. "to open their eyes, in order to turn them from darkness to light, and from the power of Satan to God, that they may receive forgiveness of sins and an inheritance among those who are sanctified by faith in Me." Acts 26:18 NKJV
15. "Therefore, if anyone is in Christ, he is a new creation; old things have passed away; behold, all things have become new." 2 Corinthians 5:17 NKJV
16. "For it is written: 'As I live, says the LORD, Every knee shall bow to Me, And every tongue shall confess to God.'" Romans 14:11 NKJV

17. "to open their eyes, in order to turn them from darkness to light, and from the power of Satan to God, that they may receive forgiveness of sins and an inheritance among those who are sanctified by faith in Me." Acts 26:18 NKJV; "In Him we have redemption through His blood, the forgiveness of sins, according to the riches of His grace." Ephesians 1:7 NKJV
18. "I can do all things through Christ who strengthens me." Philippians 4:13 NKJV
19. "But Jesus looked at them and said to them, "With men this is impossible, but with God all things are possible." Matthew 19:26 NKJV; "But Jesus looked at them and said, "With men it is impossible, but not with God; for with God all things are possible." Mark 10:27 NKJV; "The Father loves the Son, and has given all things into His hand." John 3:35 NKJV; "All things that the Father has are Mine. Therefore I said that He will take of Mine and declare it to you." John 16:15 NKJV
20. "He who did not spare His own Son, but delivered Him up for us all, how shall He not with Him also freely give us all things?" Romans 8:32 NKJV
21. "I can do all things through Christ who strengthens me." Philippians 4:13 NKJV
22. Huiothesia; www.sermonindex.net, "Adoption as sons (5206)"
23. "And suddenly a voice came from heaven, saying, 'This is My beloved Son, in whom I am well pleased.'" Matthew 3:17 NKJV
24. "Let nothing be done through selfish ambition or conceit, but in lowliness of mind let each esteem others better than himself. Let each of you look out not only for his own interests, but also for the interests of others." Philippians 2:3–4 NKJV
25. Bill Johnson (2015). "The Power That Changes the World: Creating Eternal Impact in the Here and Now," p. 54, Chosen Books
26. "Christ has redeemed us from the curse of the law, having become a curse for us (for it is written, 'Cursed is everyone who hangs on a tree.')" Galatians 3:13 NKJV; please also see Deuteronomy 28:1–48.
27. "And Jesus came and spoke to them, saying, 'All authority has been given to Me in heaven and on earth. Go therefore and make disciples of all the nations, baptizing them in the name of the Father and of the Son and of the Holy Spirit, teaching them to observe all things that I have commanded you; and lo, I am with you always, even to the end of the age.' Amen." Matthew 28:18–20 NKJV
28. "He who sins is of the devil, for the devil has sinned from the beginning. For this purpose the Son of God was manifested, that He might destroy the works of the devil." 1 John 3:8 NKJV
29. "And if we know that He hears us, whatever we ask, we know that we have the petitions that we have asked of Him." 1 John 5:15 NKJV

The Good Father

God has a heart for the lost. In Luke 15, He tells us three stories about the lost sheep, the lost coin, and the lost sons:

The Lost Sheep

"Then all the tax collectors and the sinners drew near to Him to hear Him. And the Pharisees and scribes complained, saying, 'This Man receives sinners and eats with them.'

"So, He spoke this parable to them, saying: 'What man of you, having a hundred sheep, if he loses one of them, does not leave the ninety-nine in the wilderness, and go after the one which is lost until he finds it? And when he has found it, he lays it on his shoulders, rejoicing. And when he comes home, he calls together his friends and neighbors, saying to them, "Rejoice with me, for I have found my sheep which was lost!" I say to you that likewise there will be more joy in heaven over one sinner who repents than over ninety-nine just persons who need no repentance.'"

The Lost Coin

"Or what woman, having ten silver coins, if she loses one coin, does not light a lamp, sweep the house, and search carefully until she finds it? And when she has found it, she calls her friends and neighbors together, saying, 'Rejoice with me, for I have found the piece which I lost!' Likewise, I say to you, there is joy in the presence of the angels of God over one sinner who repents."

The Two Lost Boys

Then Jesus taught the people the parable of the prodigal son. It is a beautiful story of God's love and forgiveness and has inspired many who have looked for a way home:

> "Then He said: 'A certain man had two sons. And the younger of them said to his father, "Father, give me the portion of goods that falls to me." So he divided to them his livelihood. And not many days after, the younger son gathered all together, journeyed to a far country, and there wasted his possessions with prodigal living.'"

In the Middle Eastern culture of that day, this demand by the younger son was incredibly selfish, offensive, and disrespectful. In essence, he was telling his father, "I wish you were dead!" Against all laws, customs, and courtesy, the younger son demanded his portion of the inheritance from his dad. Such disgraceful behavior would normally have been met with a left-handed slap across the face, being disowned from the family, and being ostracized by the village. As difficult as it was to cash out the estate prematurely, the chief problem being addressed in this story is not the broken law; it is the broken relationship.[1] Hurt and betrayed, the father chose not to be offended. Despite his heartbreak, he did as his son requested.

William Temple wrote, "God grants us freedom even to reject his love."[2] We witness that freedom in action as the father "still held out his broken end of the rope of relationship hoping that the other end can yet be joined."[3]

In the culture of the day, the older son would normally have rushed into the situation and mediated the dispute. Personal relationships were supremely important. Every attempt would have been made to mend this quarrel, but the text tells us that did not happen. The inference could be made by his absence that the older son was already estranged from his brother.

The story continues:

"But when he had spent all, there arose a severe famine in that land, and he began to be in want. Then he went and joined himself to a citizen of that country, and he sent him into his fields to feed swine. And he would gladly have filled his stomach with the pods that the swine ate, and no one gave him anything."

The word "prodigal" means wasteful or extravagantly spendthrift.[4] The younger son squandered his inheritance on high living and wasteful spending. He discovered that he was the center of attention with lots of friends until the party stopped, until the money ran out. He began to get very hungry, very fast. Some researchers suggest he even tried begging, but no one would help him. So, this Jewish boy found himself working for a gentile, slopping the pigs, an animal which was forbidden by his faith. Things had quickly become desperate for the boy.

"But when he came to himself, he said, 'How many of my father's hired servants have bread enough and to spare, and I perish with hunger! I will arise and go to my father, and will say to him, "Father, I have sinned against heaven and before you, and I am no longer worthy to be called your son. Make me like one of your hired servants."'"

Suddenly, the son "came to himself." I had a similar experience when, after drinking every day for sixteen years, I remember "coming to myself." I looked around the small place I had rented, living alone, and asked myself, "What are you doing here? What are you doing with your life?" This was a moment of sobriety and clarity to me, 1,000 miles away from my children, broke, jobless, and lonely. I was depressed, discouraged, and disgusted with my life.

A saint of God reached out to me and said, "God loves you and has a plan for your life." It was like cold, fresh water bringing me to my senses and stirring something deep in my heart. I needed everything God had for me. The Lord had reached out to me and showed me the way home.

In this story, the son decided to return to his village where he would beg his father to hire him as a servant. At least, he would have enough to eat. He composed his confession and began to rehearse it all the way home.

"And he arose and came to his father. But when he was still a great way off, his father saw him and had compassion, and ran and fell on his neck and kissed him. And the son said to him, 'Father, I have sinned against heaven and in your sight, and am no longer worthy to be called your son.'"

Since the boy was "a great way off," how did the father see him? Because he was looking for him. Every day, he had scanned the horizon for that familiar shape. He had heard the rumors of the villagers that the boy might be dead, but he had never given up hope. He saw his son a long way off because he was looking for him.

This is the only passage in scripture that we see God running. This is significant. God is never in a hurry; He is never shocked or taken by surprise. But when one of His lost children heads for home, all heaven holds its breath as father runs to embrace His beloved.

The word used in the passage actually means to "race."[5] Revealing his legs by lifting his robe and running was considered disgraceful and humbling. But the father didn't care what the neighbors thought, so he humbled himself before the village, his servants, and his family to save his son. His overflowing heart overruled all else as he raced to greet his boy. The two collided in embrace, kissing each other, and hugging each other tightly. Tears flowed as they spun round and round, neither wanting to ever let go.

The son caught his breath, totally surprised by the warmth, joy, and outpouring of love from his dad. He began to repent aloud, saying he was sorry and that he knew what he had done was wrong. But before he could finish his speech and ask to work as a slave, the father interrupted him and began giving orders to the staff.

> "But the father said to his servants, 'Bring out the best robe and put it on him and put a ring on his hand and sandals on his feet. And bring the fatted calf here and kill it and let us eat and be merry; for this my son was dead and is alive again; he was lost and is found.' And they began to be merry."

The father had immediately restored the young man to the family in front of the villagers who were witnessing the whole event. The robe identified the family, and wearing it symbolized the boy's standing as a son. The ring was a signet ring, used to authenticate contracts, letters, and other family business. The seal served in the same way as a modern-day signature. It allowed the bearer to act in the name and authority of the father. Sons wore sandals, while servants were barefoot.

His destiny was no longer his, as he submitted himself to his father. In this beautiful, powerful picture of God, we see ourselves. The prodigal son had presented himself as a servant, but his father received him as a son instead. In a moment of incredible forgiveness and grace, he had surrendered himself into the hands of his father, whose love triumphed over condemnation and unforgiveness. When we present ourselves to our Father as servants, He too receives us as sons instead.

Prodigals

Do you have a "prodigal" that is lost? Take heart! Our job is to pray for them, to give them a moment of clarity so they can "come to themselves." Often, people say defeatedly, "The only thing I can do is pray." The most powerful, persuasive, important thing we can do is pray! When we do, we place them in the Lord's hands, which is where they need to be because "salvation is of the Lord."[6] The Lord Himself is on the job. He knows how to draw them to Himself. After all, He saved us. It is His will, in every case, to bring them home. If you have been praying, my best advice is to buy a pair of binoculars and running shoes!

The Elder Son

> "Now his older son was in the field. And as he came and drew near to the house, he heard music and dancing. So, he called one of the servants and asked what these things meant. And he said to him, 'Your brother has come, and because he has received him safe and sound, your father has killed the fatted calf.'"

The older son had been in the field, supervising the workers. It is an interesting moment of foreshadowing that he called a servant rather than find out for himself. At this point, he got the news of his brother's return but still did not enter in.

At a celebration like this, the proper place for the oldest son was inside with his father and the guests. His responsibilities would have included serving as host for the event. But he would not take his place with the guests. When the father learned that his son was at the door, he went out to him, leaving his guests behind and bewildered.

> "But he was angry and would not go in. Therefore, his father came out and pleaded with him. So, he answered and said to his father, 'Look! These many years I have been serving you; I never transgressed your commandment at any time; and yet you never gave me a young goat, that I might make merry with my friends. But as soon as this son of yours came, who has devoured your livelihood with harlots, you killed the fatted calf for him.'"

The angry son struck a belligerent tone with his father. He cast himself resentfully as a victim, an obedient slave who had done everything demanded of him. He accused the father of favoritism by lavishing the prodigal with prime beef, while he had never received even a small goat.

Notice that he refused to even acknowledge relationship with his brother, calling him "your son" instead of "my brother." At that point, he accused his brother of spending money on prostitutes. We cannot tell from the story whether this was mean-spirited gossip or fact, but either way, he was in full attack mode. The father turned aside the boy's bitter rage and lovingly replied.

> "And he said to him, 'Son, you are always with me, and **all that I have is yours**. It was right that we should make merry and be glad, for your brother was dead and is alive again, and was lost and is found.'" Luke 15:1–32 NKJV

The father ignored the accusation and the hatred and entreated his son kindly. Notice, too, that he places the older son back into relationship with the younger son, calling him "your brother." In the spirit of grace and loving kindness, he said, "All that I have is yours." Two-thirds of the estate had already been given to the older brother to do with as he pleased. But the older son hadn't *received* what the father had given him. He didn't know what was already his. He had everything; he just didn't know it. Proud and self-centered, he demanded more and resented what little had been given to his brother.

Both sons were out of relationship with their father. The younger son had done wrong, but he had repented and humbled himself. The older son saw himself as righteous and deserving. He was filled with pride, resentment, and hatred. Both boys were lost.

We are not told the end of the story, and the relationships between the elder son and his father and brother are left unresolved. We do, however, know that in the real-life lesson, Jesus died so that both lawbreakers and law-keepers, sinners and Pharisees, grateful and ungrateful sons could enter into relationship with their heavenly father

"All Things"

In the person of the loving father in this parable, we see God. In the life of the prodigal, some of us see ourselves. We have all fallen short, made mistakes, ended up with dirty faces. And, if we have confessed our sins to Jesus, we have experienced the mercy and grace of our Lord as He restored us in relationship with Himself.

How many of us see ourselves in the older son? Have we ever become accusatory and unforgiving toward someone else? Were we the ones who stayed at home and obeyed all the rules? Has our love cooled because of perceived unfairness? Have we become self-righteous? Have we allowed a sense of duty to replace our love?

Knowing the Father's outpouring of love, greater than any offense, we may feel that tug on our hearts, calling us home, too.

There is another call. It's contained in the haunting line of the father, "All that I have is yours." What if the Lord is telling us that "all that He has" is already ours? That He has already given us "all things."

Romans 8:32 says, "He who did not spare His own Son, but delivered Him up for us all, how shall He not with Him also freely give us all things?" In other words, if God gave us Jesus, He has given us everything. Those words echo in my spirit and burn in my mind, as Father inscribes this message on our hearts: "All that I have is yours."

If that is true, if He has already provided us with *all things*, what is ours, exactly? For example, are we exercising the authority he has given us to act in his name? Do we realize we are already enrobed and enabled with the power of God? How much has been given to us that lies unclaimed? Have we laid hold of our healing? Of salvation for our family? Have we pressed the attack against the enemy in the power and authority He has already given us?

If not, why not? God forbid that we refuse to enter in where He is bidding us. Let us set aside every weight that binds us and receive everything the good Father has for us.

ENDNOTES
Chapter Three

1. Bailey, Kennth. "The Cross and the Prodigal: Luke 15 Through the Eyes of Middle Eastern Peasants." p. 61. (2005). IVP Books.
2. Ibid. p. 47.
3. Ibid. p. 53.
4. Merriam-Webster, Inc. (2018). Http://www.merriam-webster.com
5. Strong, James. "Strong's Dictionary" (1996). Thomas Nelson Publishing, Nashville, TN.
6. "But I will sacrifice to You With the voice of thanksgiving; I will pay what I have vowed. Salvation is of the LORD." Jonah 2:9 NKJV

CHAPTER FOUR

Servants and Sons

The Servant

Jesus is our perfect example of a servant. He is the King who came to serve, not to be served. He set aside His royal prerogatives, His power and privilege as the Son of God, to become a servant. Following in His footsteps, we are called to serve others as He did. The sons of God burn with the desire to serve others. That's how we rule and reign.

In the Kingdom of God, kings are servants, and servants are kings. When we esteem the needs of others above our own, we take our place as kings and priests (see Revelation 1:6). We demonstrate the sacrificial love with which Father loves us. We come in low, and the Father lifts us high. Those seeking to rule and reign must learn to serve and die.

Becoming "Unoffendable"

The Passion Translation uses a word that is not a word, but I like it anyway: "unoffendable." (Colossians 3:12, The Passion Translation). We are so *easily* offended. Our culture thrives on being offended and offending others. It is the source of ten thousand hurts and harms. Even in the church, we are easily snubbed, disappointed, disaffected, and wounded. Sometimes, it seems like we are just waiting for someone to cross us, to give us an excuse to leave in a huff. How many people do you know who have left the church because of offenses, real or imagined? How many people have shipwrecked their faith in this way? We simply need to stop being offended at every slight, especially in the body of Christ where grace should abound.

My wife is an answer to prayer, literally. As a divorced, single father, I had told God that I had given up making my own choices about dating. I always seemed to choose the wrong partners. So, I gave up and told Him it was in His hands. I was done. Through a series of impossible "coincidences," he led me to my wife, Ginger. It was completely His doing. After a year of dating, she agreed to marry me. We asked one of our pastors to marry us. But the church had a policy of not marrying people who had been divorced. We had a choice to make: either be offended and leave the church or find someone else to marry us. Our friends and our ministry were at our church, and we didn't want to leave. So, we got over it. We found someone outside the church to do our service.

This example might seem like a small matter to some, but I am fully capable of taking small matters and making them big. Left to my own, I have a talent for making mountains out of mole hills. The point is, even relatively small, emotional bumps can throw us off track if we let them. More often than not, when we are crossed, when we don't get our way, we need to get over it. In many ways, we need to get over ourselves. That is kind of what pride does; it makes our feelings, problems, and issues more important than everything else in sight.

Sooner or later, everyone gets hurt, bruised, stepped on, overlooked, rubbed the wrong way... offended. If it happened to Jesus, why do we think it won't happen to us? I tell every congregation or audience I speak to that, sooner or later, I will offend them. Those who know me nod knowingly.

If we are going to be useful in the Kingdom, we must become "unoffendable." How do we do that? First, we need to approach our lives like Jesus did, as a servant. It is impossible to offend a servant. The servant's life is not his own. His fate is in the hands of his master. His welfare, identity, and future all belong to his master.

If we do become offended and hurt, the remedy is twofold: We must continually forgive others. If we don't forgive others, God will not forgive us. Secondly, we need to fix our eyes upon Jesus, not on other people. No one has yet endured what our master endured. Whatever offense we face is less than what He faced. Our posture is that we are dead to ourselves and alive to Him. Our response to life, to living every day, to every challenge, to every person, in every circumstance, at all times, is the same: forgive them and fix our eyes upon Jesus. And don't give up.

The Throne Room Vision

Bill Johnson teaches that "if God is our servant, we will be frustrated and discouraged. But if we are God's servant, we will be continually amazed and overjoyed."[1] The mindset of the servant and the heart of the king are what are required to rule and reign in the Kingdom of God. This is the paradox of the king.

I was thinking about this during devotions one day, wondering if I was treating God as my servant, continually going to him with complaints disguised as prayer requests. Then the Lord gave me a vision. I was suddenly transported to a great throne room. It was a huge, cavernous place where God sat upon his throne. It was just Him, me, and an angel who stood beside me.

God spoke to me, "You have been seeking me, but I have been hidden from you." He asked, "What would you request of me?" As I considered how to respond, I knew, in that moment, that He would give me anything I asked. But instead of feeling overjoyed, I felt an emptiness deep inside, and I wept. Finally, I said, "To know you fully. I want to see your face. I am not satisfied with crumbs from your table, but my wish is to know you more. I want to see your face and to know you."

He did not reply for a long time, as if contemplating. An angel stood next to me. The angel said softly that my request had touched His heart. I began to sing a little song of praise. The angel said, "He has not given you the gift of singing, huh?" I laughed.

Finally, He spoke, "I will not show you my face, at least not yet. I give you my robe and scepter and ring and sandals. Whatever you ask of me, I will do. But I will not show you my face yet. Whenever you seek me, you will find me. I will not hide from you. The son may always approach the Father." Then He told me some prophecies about my future that I had hidden in my heart until that time.

Then He told me I could go. I had offered myself to Father as a servant. But instead, He received me as a son. This act of love speaks of His tenderness and kindness and power. In the Kingdom of God, the low are brought high, riches are measured by what we give away, sacrifice is gain. And servants become sons.

I believe this vision is meant for all His sons. What he gave me is available to all who call him "Father."

Robe

There are parallels between the parable of the prodigal son and my throne room experience. In the vision, Father gave me his robe. According to Scripture, the robe symbolizes a specific group or family, in this case, the royal family. Kings and priests wore costly, elaborate robes. When we wear the robe of the King, everywhere we go, people instantly recognize us as his representative.

In the Kingdom of heaven, the robe also symbolizes righteousness. The prophet Isaiah referred to the garment of salvation as the robe of righteousness.[2] For us, Jesus is our robe of righteousness. His blood is our covering. The moment we believe, we are hidden in him.

When we consider the garments of God, they all point to Jesus: the helmet of salvation, robe and breastplate of righteousness, sandals of prayer, belt of truth, shield of faith, and sword of the Spirit, which is the Word of God.[3]

Scepter

The royal scepter is a symbol of access and favor. When King Ahasuerus permitted Esther access to the throne, he extended his scepter to indicate access had been granted.[4] It showed those in attendance that he had granted a hearing. Such an occasion was powerful. If the king granted a petitioner's request, it became the law of the land. The King's decrees were carried out upon penalty of death. To have an audience with the king was the opportunity to obtain immediate answers to their petitions.

For believers, access to the throne of grace was purchased by the blood of Jesus. Once and for all, he secured us access to the Father.

There is another heavenly principle at work here. If we have access to the King, then we know He hears us. And 1 John 5:15 tells us, "And if we know that He hears us, whatever we ask, we know that we have the petitions that we have asked of Him."[5] In other words, when we have access to the throne, He hears us and grants what we ask.

To have the favor of the King on us is to enjoy preference in business relationships and open doors to new opportunities in boardrooms and conference rooms. To have favor is to walk in a place of blessing with friends, family, neighbors, and even strangers. Those with favor on them find it natural to serve others. There is a grace and peace that occurs when divine favor rests upon us.

Ring

The signet ring was like a notarized signature; it guaranteed that the enclosed orders were directly from the king. The wax imprint of the king's seal was proof that the king had issued a decree and that his power would enforce it.

Bearing the ring of the Father means that we operate in his name, in his authority. What we say goes in the realm of the king. When we speak in His name, all of His resources come to bear in strong support.

Therefore, we need to be careful about what we say. We are to speak as an oracle,[6] a mouthpiece, of God. What we speak becomes spirit and life. We bring blessing or cursing wherever we go. Life and death are in the power of the tongue.[7] And when we carry the ring, it is backed up by the authority of the King of heaven. We need to walk in the holiness and humility of that understanding.

For believers, the name of Jesus is our signet ring. He taught us that, "And whatever you ask in my name, that I will do,"[8] and, "If you ask anything in my name, I will do it."[9] And, "Most assuredly, I say to you, whatever you ask the Father in my name He will give you."[10] Whatever we ask in the name of Jesus is done. Jesus proclaimed this as truth and signed it with His life.

As believers, we carry the imprint of Him in us. We are the living insignia of our King, Jesus. He gave the sons of God such authority in order to bring heaven to earth, that the Father's will be done here, just as it is in heaven.[11] It is, therefore, incumbent upon us to say what the Father says and do what we see the Father do.[12]

Sandals

Servants go barefoot; sons wear shoes. Receiving sandals is a sign that there is a road for us to travel, that there is work to do. If we were to sit on our couches, we wouldn't need footwear.

Sandals are listed among the "whole armor of God" in Ephesians 6. Specifically, they are referred to as follows: "and having shod your feet with the preparation of the gospel of peace."[13] Our commission is to bring peace wherever we go.

Jesus is both our peace and our gospel. He is our preparation and our fulfillment. He is our everything.

Conclusion

These four items: robe, ring, scepter, and sandals, are given to the sons of men to wield influence on the earth. We are to put them on, with the whole armor of God, to do battle. This is not a defensive posture. This is offense. We are to take ground for the King and his Kingdom and occupy until He comes.[14]

In whatever sphere of influence we are in, our assignment is to carry out the orders of the King. Simply put, the message we carry is: "The Kingdom of God is within reach."[15] We are to heal the sick, cleanse the lepers (diseased), cast out demonic spirits (set people free), and raise the dead.16 Those are our marching orders.

It's time for heaven to invade earth, and the sons of God are leading the charge.

ENDNOTES
Chapter 4

1. Johnson, Bill. "Purpose Drive Life." February 23, 2016. Bethel TV. http://www.Bethel.TV
2. "I will greatly rejoice in the LORD, My soul shall be joyful in my God; For He has clothed me with the garments of salvation, He has covered me with the robe of righteousness, As a bridegroom decks himself with ornaments, And as a bride adorns herself with her jewels." Isaiah 61:10 NKJV
3. "And take the helmet of salvation, and the sword of the Spirit, which is the word of God." Ephesians 6:17 NKJV
4. "So it was, when the king saw Queen Esther standing in the court, that she found favor in his sight, and the king held out to Esther the golden scepter that was in his hand. Then Esther went near and touched the top of the scepter." Esther 5:2 NKJV
5. "And if we know that He hears us, whatever we ask, we know that we have the petitions that we have asked of Him." 1 John 5:15 NKJV
6. "If anyone speaks, let him speak as the oracles of God. If anyone ministers, let him do it as with the ability which God supplies, that in all things God may be glorified through Jesus Christ, to whom belongs the glory and the dominion forever and ever. Amen." 1 Peter 4:11 NKJV
7. "Death and life are in the power of the tongue, And those who love it will eat its fruit." Proverbs 18:21 NKJV
8. "And whatever you ask in My name, that I will do, that the Father may be glorified in the Son." John 14:13 NKJV
9. "If you ask anything in My name, I will do it." John 14:14 NKJV
10. "And in that day you will ask Me nothing. Most assuredly, I say to you, whatever you ask the Father in My name He will give you." John 16:23 NKJV
11. "Your kingdom come. Your will be done on earth as it is in heaven." Matthew 6:10 NKJV
12. "Then Jesus answered and said to them, 'Most assuredly, I say to you, the Son can do nothing of Himself, but what He sees the Father do; for whatever He does, the Son also does in like manner.'" John 5:19 NKJV
13. "and having shod your feet with the preparation of the gospel of peace." Ephesians 6:15 NKJV
14. "And he called his ten servants, and delivered them ten pounds, and said unto them, occupy till I come." Luke 19:13 KJV

15. "and saying, 'Repent, for the kingdom of heaven is at hand!'" Matthew 3:2 NKJV; "From that time Jesus began to preach and to say, 'Repent, for the kingdom of heaven is at hand.'" Matthew 4:17 NKJV; "And as you go, preach, saying, 'The kingdom of heaven is at hand.'" Matthew 10:7 NKJV; "and saying, 'The time is fulfilled, and the kingdom of God is at hand. Repent, and believe in the gospel.'" Mark 1:15 NKJV

16. "Heal the sick, cleanse the lepers, raise the dead, cast out demons. Freely you have received, freely give." Matthew 10:8 NKJV

CHAPTER FIVE

Our Inheritance

Salvation

Salvation is the birthright of sons and daughters of God. Healing, dignity, liberty, love, peace, and provision are the children's bread. Too many of us have contented ourselves with watery oatmeal instead of hearty fare. We have been starving, peering in at our own banquet.

In the original language of the Old Testament, the word used for salvation is "yeshua"[1] meaning deliverance, health, victory, and prosperity. One translation defines salvation as "deliverance from the power and effects of sin."[2] Over time, the salvation has been watered down to mean eternal life but little else. Yeshua is the Hebrew name of Jesus.[3] Yeshua is the one who delivers us from every bondage, heals us, protects us, helps us, and allows us to prosper. Our hope for today and tomorrow is in Him alone.

In the New Testament, the original Greek word for salvation is "sozo," meaning to deliver, to heal, to preserve, to be made whole, to do well. In both Hebrew and Greek, the meaning is similar. Salvation is much more than the promise of eternal life in heaven. It carries with it the fullness of life now: being free, fruitful, and victorious. The word is crystal clear that healing is for today. Prosperity is for today.

Our wholeness, body, soul, and spirit, are for today. Today is the day of salvation, the day of sozo.

If disaster were to strike, do you have peace that your destiny would be in heaven? Are you sure that God is your Father? If you don't know if you are truly saved, you can be right now. Simply ask Him to forgive you and be your savior. If you don't have the words, you can pray this prayer:

"Lord Jesus, please forgive me of my sins and be my Lord and savior."

If you have said that prayer, heaven rejoices, and eternity awaits.

Wholeness

In recent months, I have been experiencing difficulty with my memory, being unable to recall names and places. I found myself searching for the right words in the middle of sentences. Usually quick to recall stuff, I was struggling. I figured I was just getting old. Finally, it got so bad that it began to interfere with my job. I asked the Lord for help. He told me, "Fight for your mind!"

I began to search the Scriptures. I knew what it meant to stand against the enemy. I didn't need any prompting to give the enemy a black eye, but I had never heard of "fighting for my mind." Then I remembered a teaching by Kenneth Hagin, who had a testimony of having an excellent memory all his life, even into his 80s.

Hagin had read an article someone had sent him about the effects of aging on memory. From that time on, he began to have difficulty. When he prayed about the matter, the Lord told him, "You believed that article instead of my Word. My Word says you have the mind of Christ." Hagin said out loud, "I have the mind of Christ, I believe it and receive it!"[4] From that day forward, his mind was sharp as a tack. Believing and receiving are the keys to obtaining in the Kingdom of God.

I did the same thing. I bound the enemy and released the spirit of healing for my mind.[5] I declared that I had the mind of Christ! Names and places came back to me quickly, and my mind is now perfectly whole.

Neuroscientists know that the brain is not an input/output device. It is a malleable, ever-changing organ. Whether we meditate quietly or speak out loud, our words form proteins in our brains and reside there. In this way, God's Word and our words become the physical substance of our brains. Our thoughts become us. Perhaps this is one reason why the Lord teaches us to meditate upon His Word; to think on those things that are true and honest and just and beautiful (see Philippians 4:8). As we do, His Word becomes who we are, physically and spiritually.

Healing

My dear friend, Pastor Bill Napp, teaches, "When you believe man, you get what man can do. When you believe doctors, you get what doctors can do. But when you believe God, you get what God can do."

Salvation includes healing of our minds and our bodies. When we are saved, we receive blessings reserved for sons and daughters, including healing. Jesus purchased our healing for us on Calvary. That is why "by His stripes we are healed" (Isaiah 53:5). Healing is the children's bread,[6] a gift to sons and daughters. But, like all gifts, it must be received.

How, then, do we receive healing? By faith. We apprehend what He has apprehended for us by believing and receiving and then acting as if it is done.

Many fathers of our faith had anointed, powerful, healing ministries. Men and women like Smith Wigglesworth, John G. Lake, Oral Roberts, Kathryn Kuhlman, Maria Etters-Wadsworth, to name a few, operated in this gift. In this modern era, Bethel Church of Redding, California, has emerged as a place of tremendous healings, with thousands of people finding relief and wholeness. Stories abound of people being healed by just walking through the door of the church, in the very presence of the Lord. My wife and I sensed the presence of the Lord in the parking lot, for crying out loud.

My friend, Bill Napp, suffered every day for nine years with severe back pain. Four surgeries failed to give him relief. He faced a life of reduced mobility and excruciating pain. The doctors had told him there was little more they could do.

On the phone one day, he told me, "If I could get to Bethel Church, I would be healed." We decided to go. At their Saturday healing service, Bill was healed immediately and miraculously. July 16, 2019, marks the first anniversary of his pain-free life.

At the same Saturday morning healing service, I was also healed. I had lost my sense of smell ten years before on a trip to India. I received prayer from a sweet couple and thanked them for praying for me. Actually, I pointed them to my friend Bill and asked them to go pray for him, which they did. Anyway, I soon realized my sense of smell was back, fully healed.

The Lord gets all the credit and the glory for healing. It is His power at work in us. Healing is provided for His children and is promised in His Word. It is up to us to receive it and walk in it. I have come to expect Him to heal people when I pray, not because of me but because of Him. He delights in healing! He states several times that He has healed us already (see Isaiah 53:5 and 1 Peter 2:24). As a son, I have access to the Father and am able to stand on His Word as if it has already been accomplished. Because it has.

In the great moves of God through the years, there have been special outpourings of healing. The Holy Spirit has moved in specific denominations with a special anointing for healing. The Salvation

Army, Plymouth Brethren, Assemblies of God, and several other organizations have been used mightily for healing ministry. Today, the Lord is using Bethel Church in Redding, California, in this way. He has given revelation knowledge to Bill Johnson, senior pastor, and is using the staff and congregation powerfully. Nonetheless, if you can't get there (and I highly recommend visiting), the Word of God works everywhere!

I am always willing to pray with people for healing. I have seen miraculous healings on the spot, and yet, at other times, nothing seems to happen. Sometimes, people are healed several days after they received prayer; it is always not a spontaneous event. In every case, the prayer is heard and acted upon in the Kingdom of God.

A few years ago, when we were ministering in Illinois, we held coffeehouse meetings at the women's work release center in Aurora, Illinois. Larry and Karen Reckner, our ministry partners, would bring refreshments, and Ginger would lead 40 to 60 women singing and worshipping. I would usually share a brief word and then pray for anyone who came forward. One night in March, a woman named Rose came forward and asked me to pray for four specific things:

1. Her brother was getting out of prison and badly needed a job.

2. Her father had committed suicide the previous December, and the family was destitute. They needed money.

3. Her mother had stage 4 AIDS/HIV and was in the hospital under their care. They expected her to die soon.

4. She needed to get a job quickly, or she would be returned to the state prison.

So, we prayed together, packed up, and left.

When we returned in April, Rose came bounding up to us, saying excitedly, "You'll never guess what God did." I laughed and asked her to tell me. She said, "My mother is healed! The doctors could find no signs of AIDS/HIV in her, and they sent her home! Also, my brother found a job, and I did, too. And it turns out my father's wages had been garnished by the state of Illinois before he died. When his death got reported to the state, they sent my mother a check for $45,000."

The Lord just delights in showing Himself strong to those who call on Him. I just love that about Him.

Another time, an inmate came forward for prayer at the coffeehouse and asked for prayer for her children. I started to pray, and the Holy Spirit prompted me to pray for her healing, too. As soon as I prayed for healing, she started to sob. She asked, "Why did you do that?" I told her, "Because the Lord told me to." She replied, "I just came from the hospital. I had an unstoppable bleeding in my colon for six years, and they told me there was nothing more they could do for me." I told her, "Well, you are healed now, in Jesus' name!" She rejoiced and she was perfectly healed right then, right there.

Prayers are answered first in the supernatural realm and then in the natural realm—first in heaven and then on Earth. Our answer may manifest immediately, or it may take time. This is an important point. The breakthrough is always on His timetable, not ours. Once we have prayed, our job is to stand in faith, doubting nothing. We know our prayers are heard, and since they are heard, they are answered. According to Scripture, we have what we have requested.[7]

Sometimes, standing in faith means ignoring the symptoms and pain and acting as if healing had already been manifested. Our daughter, Jessie, had a severe acne problem as a teenager. It was persistent and frustrating for her that nothing seemed to work. The dermatologist told her, "There is nothing more we can do to help with this. You will have it for the rest of your life." Turning to the Lord, she and her mom prayed and asked for wisdom.

Discouraged by the doctor's report, Jessie was at the pharmacy section of the grocery store looking at the shelf of facial cleansing creams, hoping one might help. The Lord asked her, "Jessie, which one would you buy if your skin was healthy?" She thought about it and selected a gentle cleansing soap for healthy skin, which she applied with an exfoliating cloth. Later, she read Psalm 104:15, which encouraged her to use an olive oil soap and she considered an answer to prayer. Within days, her face was healed, and her skin was smooth and beautiful. Her skin condition cleared up, and she has a beautiful complexion to this day.

The gentle teaching of the Lord is so simple. There is power in acting *as if* your prayer has already been answered. Once we have prayed about a matter, Father looks to us to fulfill our part, to stand in faith before we see the answer. Our faith is exercised by acting *as if* His Word has been fulfilled, *as if* His promises have been made flesh, *as if* we have already been healed.

This is consistent with His Word. Romans 4:17 describes the power of God to "call those things which are not as though they were." And we also know that "by His stripes, we *were* healed."[8] The remedy has *already* been purchased, our hope (confident expectation) has secured the response, and our faith applies it to our current situation. We demonstrate that confidence by our words and actions. As Brother Hagin wrote, "Faith is acting *as if* God's Word is true."[9] Faith is action, the outward manifestation of our inner trust.

There is a subtle but important point regarding this scripture. Notice, it doesn't say for us to call things that *are* as though they *are not*. In other words, if sickness has struck us, then sickness has struck us. We do not deny that the issue (sickness, poverty, loss, pain, etc.) is real. What He calls us to do is speak the remedy. Speak that which we desire to occur, trusting that it is already done. Speak to the issue and tell it there is a new reality that has come. Speak to the problem, whatever it is, and tell it to bow before the name of Jesus. Tell the disease to be gone, that healing has come, because Jesus says so (by His stripes we were healed). In this way, we receive the promises He makes.

How long do we stand believing? Until. We stand until we see the answer (see Eph 6:11). Words are powerful. In the Kingdom of God, nothing happens until something is spoken. So, while we wait for healing to be manifested, we must be careful what we say. Many people have lost their healing when their words counteracted their faith. Standing in faith can deteriorate into disappointment and ineffectiveness when our mouths betray us.

When our thoughts, hearts, words, and actions are all aligned with His Word, miracles happen. Every bread maker knows that yeast takes time to "prove," to show the outward results of the inward change. Sometimes, it takes longer than others. All the scientists in the world cannot figure how long yeast needs to prove. Healing is like this. Pour your request out to the Father, stir in your faith, and wait for the mixture to "prove out."

Deliverance

For several years, Ginger and I ministered at the Wayside Cross rescue mission in Aurora, Illinois. About 128 men lived there at that time, and we volunteered, leading monthly chapel services for the men for several years. My first spiritual father was Smith Wigglesworth, the once-illiterate English plumber who was mightily used by God with a worldwide evangelical and healing ministry. Following his example, I love to exhort the men to have faith for the impossible and "only believe!"[10] One of the men, Eric, mustered up his faith and asked for prayer that his family would be reconciled and reunited. He also requested that he be delivered from drug addiction. He had been incarcerated for cocaine possession, and his wife had divorced him during his drug period. Furthermore, he was under a court-issued restraining order, forbidding him to contact his ex-wife and children in any way. No phone calls or letters were permitted. There was no way in this world for him to reach out to his family. We prayed with him, as he had asked.

We were back at Wayside a couple of months later, and he excitedly approached us, his face aglow. Frankly, he looked like a new man. "You won't believe what God has done," he said. "A week after we prayed, I got a letter from my wife, saying she wanted to talk with me. We started talking, and she wants to get back together! I have been totally clean and free from addiction. And I found a good job and can provide for her and my kids." He broke down with relief and joy over the workings of the Lord. We learned later that Eric had reunited with his family and was working as a carpenter. Eric was delivered from drug addiction and so much more.

In 1995, after I was saved, I worked temporary jobs and took my small KJV Bible to work with me. During lunch breaks, I would read and smoke. Even then, Bible passages would jump off the page at me. Some instructional, some correctional, all encouraging. The Lord frequently "highlighted" 2 Corinthian 6:17–18, which says, "Therefore, come out from among them and be separate,' says the Lord. Do not touch what is unclean [which I understood to refer to cigarettes], and I will receive you. I will be a Father to you, and you shall be My sons and daughters,' says the LORD Almighty."

After 22 years smoking two to three packs a day, I didn't really want to quit. But I was getting the message that I needed to. If I wanted to grow closer to Him and become more like Him, I would need Him to help me clean up my act. Addictions of any kind bind us to the enemy. And He loves us too much to allow the enemy to have a foothold in our lives. Satan looks for ways to find an opening in order to steal everything we have, destroy our families, and kill us (see John 10:10).

In the world, there are many masters but only one Lord. As long as I smoked, I permitted Satan to be my master. I was giving him the legal right to have his way in my life. The Lord loves us too much to allow that to continue for long, at least without a fight! His promise to me was that if I chose Him, He would be my Father, and I would be His son.

Jesus didn't die on a cross so we would remain enslaved to some other master. He endured the cross so that we could know our Father. His blood purchased our freedom to choose who we want to serve.

In service one night, the minister exclaimed that Jesus was in the room to heal. She urged whoever needed healing to touch the border of His robe. On my knees in prayer, I closed my eyes and reached up to touch the hem of His garment. I clenched my hands on the edge of His robe, believing that I could be free. In that moment, I chose God over my addiction. The Lord responded, broke my addiction, and set me free in that instant! I never craved smoking again. I had no withdrawal symptoms or desire to return to the habit. My chains were gone; it was perfect deliverance: clean, complete, without cravings or withdrawal symptoms. I call it my one-step program.

Every once in a while, I do get a stray thought to smoke. It is so odd. It always makes me laugh. Some little gremlin thinks he can sucker punch me, I guess. Usually, I just chuckle at how predictable Satan is and dismiss the thoughts. Other times, I rebuke that spirit in the name of Jesus just because I can.

The Lord did a work in me that changed me from the inside out. A whole new character had been birthed in me, and old habits passed away. All the while, He was teaching me to trust Him. Success was certain if I allowed Him to do the work. I am still going through the process—we all are. Sons and daughters are on a path of being conformed to His beauty, grace, and likeness. Faith and love are the rails on which we travel.

Peace

People often ask for prayer because of fear and anxiety. We live in a tough world. Trouble comes to all of us. Jesus understood this when He said, "In this world you will have trouble. But be of good courage for I have overcome the world."[11] As children, we do not live on our own. We have a father and a big brother to look out for us, to guard and guide us.

The cure for anxiousness and worry and the stress that accompanies them is simple. The Word teaches us to "[cast] all care upon Him."[12] We are told over and over not to worry. The remedy is to roll our cares onto our Father. It makes perfect sense. He is often the only one who can do anything about them anyway! And we were not designed to carry stress. Anxiety releases cortisol into our blood, which slowly kills us. Cortisol restricts our heart and lung activities, increases blood pressure, and leads to a host of ills. How much better to give our worries to our Father who loves us and looks out for us?

Pastor Bill Johnson teaches that many believers struggle with fear and anxiety. It is "a lordship problem."[13] He is exactly right. If Jesus is our Lord, He is big enough, capable enough, and willing to handle the anxieties of our lives. He tells us not to fear but to trust in Him.

Some tell me that is easier said than done. I do understand. I faced some serious battles. I have feared threats against Ginger and I. They paralyzed me for months. I couldn't shake them, no matter how much I prayed or confessed or repented.

Then one day, the Lord brought to mind His command to "fear not"[14] (more than nine times He instructs us to not be afraid). Suddenly, it dawned on me. If Jesus told me not to be afraid, it must be possible. I mean, He wouldn't tell me to do something I couldn't do. I understood, in that moment, that fear was a *choice*. And if Jesus told me to be unafraid, I could do it. So, I made the decision not to fear. That broke the hold that fear had on me. That was June 22, 2008. I have had a deep, abiding peace ever since.

People may say, "It can't be that easy." Actually, it is exactly that easy. If you are anxious about anything, give it to the Lord. Choose to no longer be afraid. Choose the peace of Christ. It is yours for the taking.

When I learned to solder, I used a "heat sink." This was usually a stone on which I set the burning soldering iron or the hot metals to absorb the heat. The porous stone always dissipated the heat in the metals I was soldering together. The metaphor isn't perfect, but the Lord is my "heat sink." If I have something that is too much for me, beyond my ability to handle, I give it to Him. Once I do that, I'm relieved of the issue. I place it into His capable hands. He takes all the heat.

Provision

Poverty is a curse. There is no blessing in lack. It is not a gift from God nor is it a tool He uses to make us better Christians. Besides the topic of healing, I can't think of an area of faith that has been as maligned and desecrated as that pertaining to money, which leads me to think that there is great power in the provisional principles of God. That is why the enemy seeks to discredit it so strongly.

Let's start at the top. There is a battle being waged for our souls. In bitterness and hatred, Satan is actively engaged in lying, stealing, and deceiving in order to destroy us and our families. We choose whether we will serve him or serve God. Every one of us makes this choice for ourselves. In the realm of Satan is disease, poverty, discouragement, depression, and death. In the Kingdom of God lies freedom, provision, healing, hope, love, faith, and a future. We alone choose who we will serve.

Poverty is a trap. It is, by definition, lack of necessities of life: food, clothing, shelter. It also prevents us from blessing others, from being generous. It is the opposite of an abundant life. Sons and daughters aren't to hunger after riches or chase after the stuff of this world. We don't pursue money; we pursue God. Provision comes as a blessing from a Father who loves us and cares for us. In Jesus, we always have enough and more than enough. There is no lack in God.

I have followed the Lord for 24 years. My wife and I have six children and fifteen grandchildren. I have experienced both financial disaster (my fault) and fruitful times (His outpouring). Despite my mistakes, the Lord has always provided more than enough for all of us. None of the 29 members of our immediate family has ever lacked for provision. Through fat times and thin, the Lord has always been faithful and generous and gracious to us. This same testimony is echoed millions of times within the body of Christ.

There is no lack with Father, and he doesn't use poverty and disease to discipline his children. This is a lie designed to discourage and defeat us. All good things are from Him, and there is not even a shadow of evil in Him. If there is trouble, I have learned to look for my error or the fingerprints of the enemy. The first instance calls for repentance. The second calls for warfare.

Ebenezer

In the book of Samuel, the story is told that after battling and defeating the Philistines, the prophet Samuel took a stone and named it "Ebenezer," meaning, "thus far the Lord has helped us."[15] He set it up as a memorial to Israel of the faithfulness and power of God on their behalf. Their arch enemies, the Philistines, were subdued and no longer invaded Israel. The hand of the Lord restrained the Philistines all the days of Samuel.

When the children of Israel entered the promised land, the Lord told Joshua to set up a memorial. Joshua 4:4–7 tells the story:

"Then Joshua called the twelve men whom he had appointed from the children of Israel, one man from every tribe; and Joshua said to them: 'Cross over before the ark of the LORD your God into the midst of the Jordan, and each one of you take up a stone on his shoulder, according to the number of the tribes of the children of Israel. Then you shall answer them that the waters of the Jordan were cut off before the ark of the covenant of the LORD; when it crossed over the Jordan, the waters of the Jordan were cut off. And these stones shall be for a memorial to the children of Israel forever.'"

What has the Lord done in your life? Do you have an Ebenezer, a reminder of His faithfulness and answers? Have you told your children and grandchildren about the times when He answered your prayers?

The purpose of the Ebenezer and the memorial stones was to remind the people of Israel and their children's children of the power, provision, and faithfulness of God. It is good to remember answers to prayer, especially when we are confronted with life's problems. It inspires us and the others who are watching us. The record of the Father's work in our lives also becomes our testimony.

Today, we are His memorial stones. Peter writes, "You are living stones, being built as a spiritual house..." (1 Peter 2:5). Our very lives are reminders of His goodness and power. We are called to be lively witnesses of Him.

ENDNOTES
Chapter Five

1. Strong, James. Strong's Bible Dictionary. (1996). Thomas Nelson Publishing. Nashville, TN.
2. Merriam Webster Dictionary. (2018). Merriam Webster, Inc. http://www.merriam-webster.com
3. "The Mind of Christ Doesn't Grow Old." http://www.josephprince.org
4. "And I will give you the keys of the kingdom of heaven, and whatever you bind on earth will be bound in heaven, and whatever you loose on earth will be loosed in heaven." Matthew 16:19 NKJV
5. "But He answered and said, 'It is not good to take the children's bread and throw it to the little dogs.'" Matthew 15:26 NKJV
6. "And if we know that He hears us, whatever we ask, we know that we have the petitions that we have asked of Him." I John 5:15 NKJV
7. "who Himself bore our sins in His own body on the tree, that we, having died to sins, might live for righteousness—by whose stripes you were healed." 1 Peter 2:24 NKJV
8. Hagin, Kenneth E. "The Believer's Authority." (2004). Faith Library Publications.
9. "As soon as Jesus heard the word that was spoken, He said to the ruler of the synagogue, 'Do not be afraid; only believe.'" Mark 5:36 NKJV
10. "These things I have spoken to you, that in Me you may have peace. In the world you will have tribulation; but be of good cheer, I have overcome the world." John 16:33 NKJV
11. "casting all your care upon Him, for He cares for you." 1 Peter 5:7 NKJV
12. Johnson, Bill. "The Lordship of Jesus." Video: August 11, 2019. http://www.bethel.tv.
13. Matthew 10:26, Matthew 10:28, Matthew 10:31, Luke 12:7, Luke 12:32, Romans 8:5, 2 Timothy 1:7, Hebrews 13:6, 1 John 4:18
14. "Then Samuel took a stone and set it up between Mizpah and Shen, and called its name Ebenezer, saying, 'Thus far the LORD has helped us.'" 1 Samuel 7:12 NKJV
15. Ibid.

CHAPTER SIX

Power

The Kingdom of God

Some people are accustomed to thinking of heaven when talking about the kingdom of God. Certainly, it is true that the kingdom, or "king's domain," includes the heavenly realm. But it also includes everywhere else where His authority extends. When Jesus taught "the kingdom of Heaven is at hand,"[1] He was referring to Himself. Wherever He is, so is His kingdom. Since he lives in us, wherever His sons and daughters are, the kingdom also extends to that geography, spiritually and naturally.

In the Kingdom of God, the impossible is natural. Everything the Lord ever did is still available to us today. Why wouldn't it be? The Lord doesn't change.[2] The ministries of Smith Wigglesworth, Kenneth Hagin, Oral Roberts, Bill Johnson, and many others prove this. All of the promises of God are still available to us. As sons and daughters, we have access to the Kingdom of God—all of it. And when we believe, when we trust, when we operate in the power of God, we usher in the Kingdom of heaven here on earth.

The Holy Spirit

The Holy Spirit is the power of God on earth. Once we are saved, that same Spirit who raised Jesus from the dead lives in us.[3] Deep within our hearts and minds, the Holy Spirit begins His work, transforming us from our natural state into the shining likeness of Jesus.[4]

Ephesians 1:19–23 [AMPC] puts it this way:

"And [so that you can know and understand] what is the immeasurable and unlimited and surpassing greatness of His power in and for us who believe, as demonstrated in the working of His mighty strength, which He exerted in Christ when He raised Him from the dead and seated Him at His [own] right hand in the heavenly [places], far above all rule and authority and power and dominion and every name that is named [above every title that can be conferred], not only in this age and in this world, but also in the age and the world which are to come. And He has put all things under His feet and has appointed Him the universal and supreme Head of the church [a headship exercised throughout the church], [Ps. 8:6.] Which is His body, the fullness of Him Who fills all in all [for in that body lives the full measure of Him Who makes everything complete, and Who fills everything everywhere with Himself]."

Baptism of the Holy Spirit

If you would like to receive the baptism of the Holy Spirit, ask the Father. He will do it.[5] If you know someone who speaks in tongues, ask them to pray for you to receive. Every believer has a measure of the Holy Spirit within, but not every believer speaks in tongues. Pray for the fullness of the Spirit. In the Kingdom of God, fullness means overflowing. Speaking in tongues is the overflow of the Spirit within us. Like everything else in the Kingdom realm, believe and receive, and you will have it.

The Holy Spirit is not an "it" or a "thing." The Holy Spirit is a person. He has a personality. He is the power of God and lives in us. Although He is gentle and kind, The Spirit is the most powerful force in the universe. His primary mission is to reveal Jesus to the world. On the first page of the Bible, God sent the Holy Spirit to hover over the oceans and pull them back to reveal the land masses. That's power. On the last page of the last book of the Bible, it is the Holy Spirit who cries to Jesus, "Lord, come!"[6] And He is on every page in between.

The Spirit is sensitive; He can be grieved and quenched.[7] He does not stay where He is unwelcome. Throughout history, entire denominations have enjoyed His gifts, wisdom, prophecies, and presence only to have Him move on when He was ignored or turned away. He has visited the Methodists, Congregationalists, Salvation Army, Plymouth Brethren, Assemblies of God, and Word of Faith churches through the years. Wherever He was quenched or grieved, He did not remain; He moved on.

The most important thing about Him is this: He is yours. He is not confined to any church or denomination. He is available to you for the asking. How? If you have been saved, pray to the Father saying, "Father, your Word says that you desire to give me the gift of your Holy Spirit. I believe your Word and receive Him now, in the name of Jesus." Then expect Him to be in you and with you. After all, you are the living temple of the Holy Spirit.[8]

Gifts of the Holy Spirit

The gifts of the Spirit are available to us to heal, perform miracles, see enemy spirits, reveal the truth, deeply understand the Word of God, and much more. They are always meant to reveal and honor Jesus, not to glorify us. Some of the gifts are listed in 1 Corinthians 12. They include but are not limited to miracles, healing, speaking in tongues, interpretation of tongues, discernment, faith, words of wisdom, words of knowledge, and prophecy. The Spirit operates these gifts as He decides. We don't need to "work them up."

There is no limit to the power of God. He gives gifts and talents to people as blessings to them. Gifts of wisdom and understanding, of empathy and intelligence, of language and business abound. Talents for music and art, math and science, speech and writing are all around us. Spirits of liberty, peace, wisdom, and other godly attributes are freely distributed. The goodness of God is manifest everywhere. God is a great and generous Father. The Lord also gives gifts of visions and dreams. Some daughters and sons are gifted as seers. They are given glimpses of the future or spiritual revelations. Those with a gift of prophecy are told of things to come. Others with a gift of discernment see into the spiritual realm. Gifts of the Spirit are given to edify, or build up, believers to strengthen the church. They are not given as personal trophies or rewards. They are given for the benefit of other believers.

God gives everyone gifts. 1 Corinthians 7:7 says, "But each one has his own gift from God, one in the manner and another in that." Also, Ephesians 4:8 says, "When He ascended on high, He led captivity captive, and gave gifts to men." Every good gift is from God (see James 1:17). And if we, being earthly fathers, "know how to give good gifts to [our] children, how much more will [our] Father in heaven give good things to those who ask Him!" (Matthew 7:11). Seek Him and all that He has for you. What gifts and talents has He given you?

Praying in Tongues

Those who have been baptized in the Holy Spirit can pray in tongues. This is a private prayer language, known to Father. When we start to pray in our own language, the Spirit takes over, and we pray in a language that is not ours. When we do, we unleash praise, petitions, intercession, adoration, and words of power and faith that we don't even know we have! Our spirit connects directly with the Holy Spirit in communion and communication that is powerful, quickening, and uplifting.

There is also a spiritual gift of speaking and interpreting unknown tongues. These are different gifts than the private prayer language discussed above. These gifts involve someone having a message from God in an unknown language with someone present who can translate what it means. In a group setting, prophecies are often delivered this way. This is a public occasion, not a private one. The Lord uses these gifts to encourage and strengthen the assembled believers.

What if we don't know what to pray for? We are told, in such cases, to yield ourselves to the Holy Spirit and let Him pray through us. He gives us the words to say. When praying this way, we usually don't know what the words mean, but we do know that He is using us to intercede in situations and on behalf of people who need prayer. Imagine being used by God to intercede on behalf of someone who needs help, whom you have never met. It is a powerful deal.

Just to be clear, it's not necessary for us to know what is being prayed about. The Spirit gives us utterance as He wills. In yielding to Him in this spiritual task, we accomplish the will and purposes of God.

Those who are Spirit-filled know that praying in tongues is beautiful, powerful, and effective. We know this because it is not us who controls the prayer language, it is the Spirit of God. He controls our tongue in prayer. Neuroscientists have imaged the portion of the brain that is activated when someone is speaking in tongues. Interestingly, it is not the speech function that is triggered. It is the portion of the brain that is engaged as our "spiritual center," which we use when we think of God and spiritual matters.

Endnotes

Chapter Six

1. "From that time Jesus began to preach and to say, 'Repent, for the kingdom of heaven is at hand.'" Matthew 4:17 NKJV
2. "Jesus Christ is the same yesterday, today, and forever." Hebrews 13:8 NKJV
3. "That good thing which was committed to you, keep by the Holy Spirit who dwells in us." 2 Timothy 1:14 NKJV
4. "But we all, with unveiled face, beholding as in a mirror the glory of the Lord, are being transformed into the same image from glory to glory, just as by the Spirit of the Lord." 2 Corinthians 3:18 NKJV
5. "If you then, being evil, know how to give good gifts to your children, how much more will your heavenly Father give the Holy Spirit to those who ask Him!" Luke 11:13 NKJV
6. "He who testifies to these things says, 'Surely I am coming quickly.' Amen. Even so, come, Lord Jesus!" Revelation 22:20 NKJV
7. "Do not quench the Spirit." 1 Thessalonians 5:19 NKJV
8. "Or do you not know that your body is the temple of the Holy Spirit who is in you, whom you have from God, and you are not your own?" 1 Corinthians 6:19 NKJV

Prayer

Answers

We all want the same thing. We want to get our prayers answered. We look for prayers that "work." We want a system that is repeatable, dependable, and predictable. The trouble is, God doesn't work that way. So, how can we pray and know that we have been heard? How can we get results?

There is one absolute rule about prayer: There is no absolute rule about prayer. There is no formula with the Father. God does as He pleases.[1] He is not bound to follow the traditions and dictates we set out. In fact, He seems to go out of His way to demolish every box we try to put Him in. He breaks out all the time. He will not be constrained or contained. He is God.

Even still, every cry from our heart to Him is heard. If we need help, if we need our Father to act on our behalf, we cry out to him. There is no one "right way" to seek Father. Build a relationship with Him. Find your own best way to talk with Him. He loves you. He loves to hear from you. And He loves to show Himself strong to his children. As Mark Batterson writes, "Sometimes God shows up, and sometimes He shows off!"[2] Enjoy your time with Him! It will be a source of peace, of intimacy, and deep communion with the one who loves you more than life. Watch Him "show off" in your life in unique and powerful ways, just for you. God delights in delighting you.

The "secret" lies in entering into a relationship with Him, getting to know Him. Effectual prayer has a lot to do with our relationship with Father. Everything flows from that. And the central issue lies not in what we want but what God wants. Surrender and yieldedness are crucial to knowing Him. Are we serving Him or expecting Him to serve us?

Hearing from Father

The beauty of the dawn and the sparkling of the night sky reveal Him to a waiting world. He says, "day after day utters speech and night after night speaks knowledge"[3] of Him. This is the God who is always speaking. His Spirit is in contact with our spirits. He speaks to us, sometimes in audible ways, other times in our minds. His voice may sound like our voices, but His thoughts are not our thoughts.[4] I can tell when He speaks to me because He tells me things I don't know. I couldn't do that myself.

I hear Father most clearly when reading His Word and in prayer. The Bible is His Word. It is Jesus in print. Every believer I know has had the experience of certain passages "jumping off the page." That is the Spirit of the Lord quickening us, highlighting a certain segment of His Word. In those moments, the Bible comes alive. We gain instant understanding and application to our specific needs. The Word answers our deepest questions, spoken and unspoken. I am often asked which version is the "best." The answer is, the one we can understand most clearly.

In prayer, I have found that one of the most difficult things to do is to quiet myself, to stop the internal dialogue and be still. Then I can hear. When my mind is racing and thoughts and conversations and images are marching through my consciousness, I cannot focus on Him.

While it is true that God is everywhere and always available, there is something precious about having a quiet place set aside, a prayer closet, to meet with Him. Anyway, there are some simple ways to stop the internal dialogue, to focus on the Lord. Find a place to pray apart from noise, distractions, and people. This can be beside a bed or sofa or chair. The important thing is to find a time and place to focus solely on Him, away from the distractions of life.

He breaks through our daily routines whenever He wants! He has spoken to me in many places, such as airplanes, rental car lots, and in my car. But when I want to seek Him, I need to focus. I need to stop the clamor of the world from ringing in my ears. Multitasking just doesn't cut it. I cannot pray while driving. Although, if you saw my driving, it might help your prayer life. And I don't want to say, "pray in this place but not in that place." We are all busy, and sometimes, we have an urgent need, and we send it up to Father. I get it.

I look for time and a space where I can be undisturbed. I get on my knees. This is a posture of humility. I focus my thoughts by praising Him and thanking Him for what He has done for me and my family. As I recall answers to prayer, it reaffirms my faith and charges the atmosphere. Often, I pray out loud because the power of my testimony reverberates through the atmosphere and sets the stage for more. I search my heart and conscience for anything that might stand between us. I check and see if I need to forgive anyone. By this time, He is already present; He is with me. Many times, my prayer list drops to the floor, and I just revel in Him.

He teaches, corrects, encourages, and warns. I have learned to write those things down, to meditate on His Words, as they are extraordinarily helpful. I have learned that He does not repeat himself. He expects me to do what He has already said. He expects me to remember what He has told me to do and to be obedient. Until then, I am almost never able to move beyond that point. Sometimes, this requires me to go back to the last thing He told me to do and make sure I have done that. To pick up where I left off and to obey. Only then can I move forward with Him.

A large measure of hearing and obeying is familiarity and trust. Are we sure we are hearing His voice? Do we know His voice well enough to trust Him? Are we spiritually in tune with the Father? The answer to these questions lies in experience. We need to spend enough time with the Father that we recognize His voice, that we know His call. There are lots of voices in the world and, sometimes, in our heads. How do we single out His? By knowing His voice and His will.

When we visit our daughter and son-in-law's farm, we often visit their sheep. I have tried calling them, looking for a response, but they just lie there, chewing their cud, staring at me. But when my son-in-law Josh speaks to them, they suddenly jump to their feet and are on the move. The difference is that they know his voice. They respond to the call of their shepherd.[6]

We need to spend time with God to know His voice. The first place to start is prayer. The second is listening. To me, His voice sounds like my voice except what He tells me is really smart. His thoughts are always different than my thoughts. Over time, I have learned to pick out His voice from the crowd. He has a distinct, quiet, but authoritative tone. He doesn't holler and fuss in my ears. He speaks, I listen, my spirit bears witness with His Spirit, and I know it is Him.[7]

Often, our Father speaks softly. He is not controlling; He is not a bully. Father does not force Himself or manipulate us in any way. The creator of heaven and earth is a gentleman and waits for us to turn toward Him. He knows how to get our attention.

Our bodies have voices too, and they can be loud. My stomach, for example, has a voice of its own and can be pretty demanding. It speaks the language of jelly doughnuts. My will and pride also want to be heard. But becoming sensitive to the leading of the Holy Spirit is a key factor in growing up spiritually. It helps us discern what the Lord wants in any given situation. It is also a warning system against the spirit of error, manipulation, control, and danger.

Some people think it is weird that God speaks to me. I think it would be weird if He didn't. After all, He is my Father. What father wouldn't speak to his son? With the Holy Spirit living inside me, I have a direct spiritual connection to the Father. I can hear Him, feel His nudges, sense His presence, and sometimes see His hand at work. When I hear His voice, there is no doubt that it is His voice and not my own. He speaks with authority and tells me things I don't know. He reserves these encounters to tell me something new to accomplish His purposes.

When we do services in jails, I ask Father what He wants me to tell the men and women. He always tells me, "Tell them I love them." Often, he adds a special word for them. And whenever I speak that word to them, the Holy Spirit sweeps across the room and lands in the hearts of those for whom it was sent. I have seen huge, tough, rock-faced guys become undone at a word from the Lord. Before a recent service, the Lord told me, "Tell them I love them and that I have found the way home." I didn't understand the message. After all, God didn't lose His way or forget where heaven was. It made no sense to me. I was concerned that I had heard Him wrong, but I delivered the message anyway.

As I spoke it, we could see the Holy Spirit sweep across the room. The inmates were deeply affected. Through their tears, 51 of those men asked Jesus to be their savior. He knew exactly what would touch the hearts of those guys. More than 90 percent of those in jail are men. And 75 percent of them have grown up without fathers.[8] The Lord was calling out to those men, bringing them home to a father they never knew.

In a chapel service for the women inmates, the Lord told me to tell them He loved them and that "they were not forgotten." The room melted in tears of repentance and joy. Several confessed their worst fears that their children had forgotten them. Imagine their grief. They were deeply moved to discover that Father knew their deepest pain and assured them that they were not forgotten.

Recently, He gave me a word that I was sure I misunderstood. He said, "Tell them that I love them and will do anything for them." That sounded pretty far-fetched, something I might have made up or heard wrong. I asked Him again, but He did not repeat Himself. Nor did he substitute anything else more to my liking. I thought. "Really, Lord? You are willing to do anything for these guys? They can come up with a long list of wants. Truthfully, I was concerned with looking bad. You know, because I had it all figured out. What if they responded with something ridiculous, something crazy, like, "break me out of jail" or "I want a million dollars?"

I told them that there are two kinds of people in the world, enemies of God and sons. And they choose which group they belong to. For sons, the Father stood ready to hear and act on their behalf and to perform His Word, including "doing anything they asked." I told them what Father told me. The effect was immediate. What I worried was stupid turned into something extremely powerful. More than 100 men and women came to four jail services that Sunday afternoon, and 52 men and women were saved.

There will be times when Father tells us something that doesn't make sense to us. The question is, will we be surrendered and obedient in that moment? Are we willing to set aside our right to understand and control everything? Are we willing to risk looking foolish and speak His words of wisdom and power?

Thanksgiving and Praise

"We enter His gates with thanksgiving and come into His courts with praise," says Psalm 100. As Pastor Bill Johnson teaches, "Thanksgiving reminds us of what He has done. Praise reminds us of who He is."[9] Powerful lesson, that. Nothing helps us enter His very presence more than praising Him for who He is. Not because He needs to hear it, but because we do. We need to remind ourselves who He is, of His lordship over all.

Praise also ushers in His presence. Why? Because the Lord "inhabits the praises of His people."[10] Strengthened by a heart of thankfulness and quickened by the spirit of praise, we arrive "boldly before the throne of grace." We find ourselves in His very presence with our requests empowered by faith and our hearts grateful to receive. Thanksgiving and praise are the turbojets of prayer. They transport us directly in front of Him. And if we know that our prayers are heard, then we also have confidence that they are answered (see 1 John 5:15).

Thanking God for hearing and providing *before* we see the answer is a great way to start. Give Him praise *as if* He had already answered. By thanking Him in advance, it reveals our confident expectation in Him. It announces our trust in Him. Thankfulness is the trumpet blast that shouts that the walls have fallen down.

Is it honest to thank God for doing something you haven't seen happen yet? Sure, the Lord does it. In Romans 4:17 he tells us to call "those things which are not, as though they were." It is a legal request. He did it as our example. He called Gideon a mighty man of God even while his knees were knocking. He said, "Let the weak say I am strong."[11] Jesus called Peter a solid "rock"[12] upon which He would build the church, even though he was as squirrelly as he could be, denying that he even knew Jesus.[13]

Before we even pray about our needs, Father is already ordering and reordering the universe (see Matthew 6:8, Isaiah 65:24). It seems only fitting to thank Him for answering our prayers before we utter them. He teaches us that, before our knees hit the floor, He is already on the move, providing what we need.

Faith

Bill Johnson teaches that God's arm is not moved by great need—it is moved by great faith.[14] If God was moved by great need, people would not die of disease, children would not die of starvation, nor would communities be devastated by floods, hurricanes, and earthquakes. But the fact is, God is moved by faith. It is by faith that entire countries are raised up or destroyed, the dead raised to life, and the sick healed. It is by faith that people are saved, lives transformed, shackles released, and the gospel spread. Faith in God heals, provides, protects, saves, and sets us free. Faith is the path that leads to our Father in heaven and eternal life.

Everything in the Kingdom of God works by faith and love. There is nothing we receive from our Father that hasn't been purchased by love and delivered in faith.

From time to time, I get fed up and disheartened with the acidic political environment and the decay of civility and kindness in the world. Ginger reminds me of what her dad, a WWII pilot and pastor used to teach: "This world is the perfect testing ground for your faith." Every difficulty is an opportunity to exercise our faith. As my friend Don Davenport says, every illness or setback or need has a supernatural tag on it that says "[insert faith here]." Faith is the key that unlocks the door. Finally, Lilian Yeomans wrote beautifully that "faith is the hand that receives the gift from God."[15]

God gives every one of us enough faith to get the job done.[16] Everyone has enough faith to be saved, for example. It is deposited in our hearts from God. Once we are saved, our faith grows by hearing and reading the Word of God.[17] I have found that nothing increases my faith more strongly than hearing Father speak to me. His voice, presence, and teaching fills me with ever-increasing faith in Him.

Reading the Word increases our faith. It causes us to trust Him more and more. Every book in the Bible is a faith-builder. Matthew, Mark, Luke, and John reveal Jesus and speak of forgiveness and sacrifice. Philippians teaches us to meditate on the present and forget the past.[18] Galatians teaches us about dying to self and becoming alive to Him.[19] Hebrews reminds us of the heroes of our faith and what they did, despite all odds. It challenges us to do what they did. 1 Corinthians teaches about the gifts of God and how to live in love. The whole New Testament is an anthem to His great love and faithfulness.

Mark 11:22 delivers a stunning insight into faith. Young's Literal Translation puts it this way:

> "And Jesus answering saith to them, '*Have faith of God;* for verily I say to you, that whoever may say to this mount, be taken up, and be cast into the sea, and may not doubt in his heart, but may believe that the things that he saith do come to pass, it shall be to him whatever he may say. Because of this I say to you, all whatever—praying—ye do ask, believe that ye receive, and it shall be to you.'" Mark 11:22–24 YLT, 1898

This scripture tells us to pray with God's faith, not ours. In other words, as sons and daughters, we have access to the Father's level of faith, which is total. The Complete Jewish Bible makes it even clearer: "Pray with the trust that only comes from God." What would happen if we approached our prayer list with the trust that comes from Father Himself? Mountains would crumble. This is a key to effective prayer.

Many of us try to muster up enough faith to be heard and answered. It is a frustrating and useless exercise. We have all done it. No amount of begging, pleading, demanding, or bargaining impresses the Lord. What moves the hand of God is our quiet trust in Him. Period. It is our willingness to turn the tiniest amount of faith, as little as a tiny seed, toward Him. When we tell Him that we trust Him to be on our side, to do what's best for us, to fulfill His Word in our lives, He moves heaven and earth on our behalf.

That is faith.

Ginger and I taught our ladies at the Illinois Department of Corrections work release center about Mark 11:22. One of them, Linda, had recommitted her life to the Lord and faithfully came to every chapel service and Bible study we did for two years. She had grown dissatisfied working for minimum wage at an entry-level job and wanted to get her nursing license reinstated. The challenge was, she had been arrested and sentenced for manufacturing and distributing crystal meth. The health authorities had suspended her license when she was convicted of her crime. To make matters more complicated, her nursing license was from the State of Indiana, and she wanted to work in Illinois. To the best of our knowledge, no state had ever reinstated a nursing license for a felon while still incarcerated and then granted reciprocity from another state.

But Linda believed in a miracle-working God, and so did we. So, we prayed according to Mark 11, speaking our faith aloud. We waited expectantly for a miracle. We didn't have to wait long. Within a few weeks, the State of Indiana granted her request and reinstated her nursing license. Then, against all odds, Illinois recognized the reinstatement and reissued her nursing license! Linda served out her time with the Department of Corrections working as a licensed nurse in a nearby nursing home.

Baby Joel

Our daughter, Jennifer, has given us a miracle grandson named Joel. This is her story:

At 35 years old, a divorced mother of three, I had no intentions of having any more children—ever. So, on March 14, 2014, during a time of prayer journaling, I felt God prompt me to write that His plans were to "keep an open mind and an open heart. You will bear a son. Joel," I dropped my pen, then scoffed a little. "God," I wrote, "you're totally gonna have to reiterate this one for me—I'm having a hard time swallowing it." "So did Sarai," He said. Bluntly, I didn't want it.

In July of 2015, Martin and I were married. In October, I contracted a particularly virulent respiratory infection that required some strong antibiotics. I then had some of the more major side effects, which landed me in the ER. During that visit, they wanted to do a CT scan of my chest to ensure that the infection hadn't spread to my heart. In their due diligence prior to the CT, they did a serum pregnancy test, which came back positive. Having been so sick and on such strong medications, I had very mixed emotions about this news. I still really wasn't excited to be pregnant, and I was scared that the baby may have been harmed by all the meds. Later that day, I was discharged home with a pregnancy-friendly plan to heal and rest. In the weeks that followed, as I spent a lot of time resting and recovering, I began to accept the fact that I was pregnant and even started to get a little excited! When we told our five children the news, the youngest, Ethan (12) was less than thrilled. He pouted while the rest of us discussed what it would be like to add a baby to the family, and the subject of names was brought up. Several names were suggested, including my offer of Greyson. The guys thought since we had an Isaiah "Z-man" and an Ethan "E-man," it might be fun to add "G-man" to the mix. Ethan, still pouting, raised his head and said, "Wait, what about... eh, never mind," and hung his head again. Trying to encourage him to participate, my husband prodded him.

"Well, I can't really explain why, but for some reason I've just really always liked the name Joel."

My jaw dropped. I had never told my children about the prayer journal entry. I rushed down to the basement to find the journal and brought it up to show Ethan. The color left his face. Wonder, faith, and utter shock flashed across his face as he marveled, "Did God just use me?" Our family prayed together, thanking God for this beautiful moment and for the sweet little life growing inside me. We sent out pregnancy announcements as our Christmas cards and started preparing to welcome our little Joel.

A few days before Christmas, at our annual family Christmas cookie exchange party, I began having some cramping. I cancelled my shopping trip the next day, knowing my body was telling me I needed to rest, but as the day progressed, symptoms worsened, and I began to fear that something was wrong. We went back to the ER; they ordered an ultrasound. The look on the tech's face told me that my fears were confirmed. They could not detect a heartbeat. I was discharged home again, this time with instructions to wait for my body to complete the miscarriage.

The next few days and that Christmas are a blur, but a couple of days after Christmas, grieving and full of hurt and confusion, my husband and I decided to get small tattoos on the inside of our left wrists memorializing Joel. We selected a simple drawing of a sleeping baby angel, and as we waited in the tattoo parlor, Martin suggested that we add a Bible verse to the design. I knew Joel was a book in the Bible, but I couldn't immediately recall any specific verses from that book, so I opened up the Bible app on my phone and began scanning the chapters. "Here, how about this one?" I said. "Joel 2:25 says, 'So I will restore to you the years that the swarming locust has eaten....'"

Martin asked what that meant to me. "Well, I think it's saying that God will restore to us what the devourer has taken." So, Joel 2:25 became my tattoo that late December day of 2015.

I spoke with my mom about the continuing loss I felt and not understanding where the Lord was as things had unfolded. She told me, "Jenny, that wasn't Joel. That baby you carried and lost... it wasn't Joel. The Lord's promises always come to pass. If He told you that you would have a son named Joel, then you will!"

A year later, I found out I was pregnant again. I was excited this time! I told my husband, and we both were thankful that God was making good on His promise, but being a little bit gun-shy, we kept the news largely to ourselves. We didn't tell the kids, we didn't tell our parents. No announcements were sent, but things seemed to be progressing pretty normally. My doctor had examined me, said everything looked good, and scheduled an ultrasound. We were in a different office with a different tech, but that same look came across her face. She went to get the doctor, and after looking at that screen for a painfully long time, he explained to me that sometimes, when a defect of some sort is detected shortly after conception, the baby will stop developing, but the body still allows the "pregnancy" to progress. He called it a blighted ovum. There was no baby in my womb. I felt gypped. Nine weeks of hope. Nine weeks of perceived bonding. Nine weeks of being so careful with everything that went into my body. Nine weeks of sickness and soreness that I had withstood willingly, knowing that I would have a wonderful reward when it was over.

In my mind, I think I was sort of prepared for the possibility of another miscarriage, but to hear that there had never even been a baby? That just felt cruel. On top of that, I needed to have a D&C to clear out the remnants and reset my body. This was right before Christmas, again. At the hospital for the surgery, the mood was somber. Everybody was sorry. I felt so cold. I was discharged home, yet again, to heal. But this time, the emotional wounds hurt so much worse than anything I was feeling physically. I got home and got in the shower, and I cried. I cried harder than I think I've ever cried. My soul groaned.

"God, I don't understand this. I can't feel You in this. Why would You promise this and then take it away?" I broke. I fell to my knees in the shower and, still sobbing, cried out to my Father. "God, I *know* that You are good, even though I can't see it. I *know* that You are in control, even though I can't feel it. I *know* that You keep Your promises, even when I can't see how. God, You are still good. You are still worthy. God, I praise you anyway, and God, I *trust* Your plan. Blessed be Your name!"

Six months later, I had another positive pregnancy test. I didn't let myself really believe it. I waited a few weeks to even tell my husband. We made it through our first doctor's appointment and even passed the first ultrasound with flying colors. We went home with photos that day and an estimated due date of February 19, 2018. Weeks passed. Things all looked good! We had multiple ultrasounds that all looked, and I quote, "perfect." We managed to wait until almost [20] weeks before we announced the pregnancy to our families.

Fast-forward to February. My husband's dream of having a Valentine's Day baby came and went. Our due date came and went. I had been having some contractions at my doctor's appointment, so he sent me up to Labor & Delivery to be monitored for a couple of hours. The baby was having some heart rate decelerations with each contraction, so my doctor was encouraging me to be induced. I had been induced with all three of my big kids, and I really was hoping to have a naturally progressing labor, but I was considering my doctor's advice. However, my contractions stopped, and baby's heart rate normalized. It was a Thursday, so I bargained with my doctor—if I didn't go into labor naturally over the weekend, he could induce me Monday morning. As I was putting on some lotion the next day, I rubbed over the inside of my left wrist. I remembered the promise. I remembered the losses. I remembered the verse. The Lord will restore what the devourer has taken. Joel 2:25. I looked at the calendar. It was 2/23.

Sunday morning, I was awakened by a painful contraction. I glanced at the clock. It was 2:25 a.m. Around 7:00 a.m., things were progressing, so we headed into the hospital. The labor and delivery floor was completely full. We were parked in an exam room to labor. As things intensified, it became clear that we were getting close, and thankfully, a birthing room opened up just in time. They got the room cleaned quickly and hurried us down the hall and casually mentioned we were going to room 225. My husband and I exchanged glances.

On 2/25/2018 at 9:25 a.m., we welcomed our precious baby boy, Joel Greyson Ellis into this world. Complete joy, perfect fulfillment, and pure love were cherished. Oh, and we were discharged from the hospital at 2:25 p.m. Our joy was complete, promise fulfilled.

Praying His Word

A. W. Tozer wrote that faith is simply bringing ourselves into alignment with the Word of God.23 There is nothing more powerful than praying what He has said. For example, when we pray, "by His stripes we are healed" we are quoting Isaiah 53. We are coming into agreement with what He has already proclaimed. We are coming alongside God in agreement. What could be more powerful than partnering with the creator of heaven and earth? To align ourselves with what the Father is doing and saying turbo-charges our prayers. Our prayers become God-breathed. And if they are God-breathed, they are God-powered.

The scriptures are clear that we are not to pray using "vain repetition,"24 the same empty phrases over and over. We should not come before Him simply repeating ourselves. If you don't know what to pray, pray God's prayers. Ephesians chapters 1 and 3 contain powerful, profound, anointed prayers. Insert your name in the place of me, our, or my. Make them personal, make them yours. Watch as your faith is fanned to open flame:

Ephesians 1

"...that the God of our Lord Jesus Christ, the Father of glory, may give to you the spirit of wisdom and revelation in the knowledge of Him, the eyes of your understanding being enlightened; that you may know what is the hope of His calling, what are the riches of the glory of His inheritance in the saints, and what is the exceeding greatness of His power toward us who believe, according to the working of His mighty power which He worked in Christ when He raised Him from the dead and seated Him at His right hand in the heavenly places, far above all principality and power and might and dominion, and every name that is named, not only in this age but also in that which is to come." Ephesians 1:17–21 NKJV

Ephesians 3

"For this reason I bow my knees to the Father of our Lord Jesus Christ, from whom the whole family in heaven and earth is named, that He would grant you, according to the riches of His glory, to be strengthened with might through His Spirit in the inner man, that Christ may dwell in your hearts through faith; that you, being rooted and grounded in love, may be able to comprehend with all the saints what is the width and length and depth and height—to know the love of Christ which passes knowledge; that you may be filled with all the fullness of God. Now to Him who is able to do exceedingly abundantly above all that we ask or think, according to the power that works in us, to Him be glory in the church by Christ Jesus to all generations, forever and ever. Amen." Ephesians 3:14–21 NKJV

We are to come to the Father in "spirit and in truth." (see John 4:24). We need to be sincere in prayer and honest with ourselves about our motives. In fact, Father looks for such sons and daughters to hear their prayers, answer their cries, and to spend time with them. He desires a warm, loving relationship with us, even more than we do with Him.

Praying His Will

The Lord gave us a powerful promise in 1 John 5:14–15:

"Now this is the confidence that we have in Him, that if we ask anything according to His will, He hears us. And if we know that He hears us, whatever we ask, we know that we have the petitions that we have asked of Him."

How do we know His will? We know because He has written it in His Word. I like to look for the "always" statements in the Bible. When it comes to hearing from the King, absolutes are rare and powerful. The promises of God are always "Yes" and "Amen!" (2 Cor 1:20). Find a promise of God; there are several thousand in the Bible.

Write them down.

Read them out loud.

Make them yours (personalize them).

Pray over them.

Trust God for them.

Thank God for answering your prayers while you wait.

See the results.

Alpha and Omega

God exists outside of time. He tells us that He is the "Alpha and Omega,"[21] the beginning and the end. In other words, He knows the beginning and end of our timeline and everything in between. Herein lies another paradox. If human history has already been written (and it has), how can there be free will? If we are, indeed, free to make choices, thousands a day, how can the end result already be known? This question confounds philosophers, theologians, and everyone else. On the surface, it appears to be an unsolvable paradox. But, as we know, the Kingdom of God is home to paradox.

When we pray, God has already looked ahead and seen our future. He knows what we will need tomorrow. He then reorders resources and relationships to provide all that we will need. Before we even ask for it, He is on the job making it happen on our behalf. Amazing God.

Recently, Ginger pointed out to me a baby robin in a nest in our backyard. He was alone in the nest with his beak open, chirping up a storm. He spent all day squawking and working his beak in hopes that his mother or father would fill it. All the while, we could see the mother robin busily at work, catching worms.

As I was praying and bringing my "petitions"[22] before him, He flashed that scene in my mind. I was just like that baby bird, chirping away at Father, looking to be fed. Unbeknownst to me, He was already on the job, providing, protecting, and looking ahead for all that I would need. I laughed out loud.

Praying Specifically

Pastor Paul Yonggi Cho was the senior pastor of the largest Christian church in the world, Yoido Full Gospel Church in Seoul, South Korea. He taught that praying specifically is powerful in the Kingdom of God.20 In twenty years of ministry, Ginger and I have also found this to be true. When we are specific in prayer, we recognize the answer when we see it! Vague prayers yield vague answers. Maybe God heard me, maybe He didn't. What a frustrating exercise. Vague prayers do not build faith. However, when we pray specifically, we know when He answers and can give Him the glory for it.

As Laurie was nearing the end of her sentence, she and her husband, just released from prison, needed a home for their family. Laurie decided to trust God for a very specific answer. She prayed for a house to rent in southern Illinois, in the country, with a long gravel driveway, and attached garage. She asked for a washer and dryer on the first floor, four bedrooms, and rent less than $450 per month.

After looking for a while, her husband called, excitedly reporting that he had found the perfect place for $600 a month. But it did not have a garage nor a washer and dryer. She told him, "That is not the right place for us." Frustrated and a little miffed, her husband reluctantly agreed to continue the search. Within a few days, he called again and told her the incredible news. He had found a house in the country with an attached garage and long gravel driveway. It had four bedrooms and two sets of washers and dryers, one set in the basement and one on the first floor. Furthermore, it was only $430 per month! The Lord had answered her prayer; she knew it was the right place, and they rejoiced.

One day, she asked us to pray for her 16-year-old daughter. She had been on the run from authorities, and no one had heard from her for three weeks. That Sunday morning, around 10:00 a.m., we prayed for her safety and that she would contact her mom. At 11:30

a.m., the payphone rang in the facility. It was Laurie's daughter. She had turned herself in to the sheriff's office and was seeking help. Laurie's prayers were answered. The Lord showed Himself strong to her and her family at every turn, and her faith grew and triumphed repeatedly.

Recently, I decided I "needed" a new pickup truck. So, I called my buddy Don in the used vehicle department and told him what I was looking for. He told me that he had seen nothing come into the dealership. Then, a couple of weeks later, I decided to ask specifically and told him to be on the lookout for a late model Toyota Tundra, superwhite, with low mileage, 6.5' bed, good price, WeatherTech floor mats, and all the technology. He texted me, "It came in yesterday." Knowing our previous conversation and that these were hard to find, I told him that "he didn't understand." I wanted a late model Toyota Tundra, superwhite, with low mileage, 6.5' bed, good price, WeatherTech floor mats, and all the technology. He said, "You don't understand. It came in yesterday. I haven't even entered it into the inventory sheets yet, and it's not advertised." He then texted me a picture of the WeatherTech floor mats to prove my request had been answered in every detail!

Father had answered prayer *before* I had even asked. I knew it wasn't chance or accident because it was a perfect answer to a specific request. Father was showing off again. And I was amazed. Again.

Delay

I cannot speed up God's answer to prayer, but I can slow it down.

Sin, carnal desires, wayward requests that are inconsistent with His Word, unbelief, unforgiveness, and being double-minded can prevent Him from answering our prayers altogether. Prayer is the perfect time for an honest gut check. Psalm 138:23 says, "Search me, O God, and know my heart; try me and know my anxieties; and see if there is any wicked way in me..." This is always a safe place to stand in prayer.

I can prevent God from answering my prayers if I fail to forgive others.[25] If I am holding a grudge or have become bitter with someone, He won't forgive me. Conversely, forgiving others releases God to forgive us. His instructions are crystal clear: "Go make it right with your brother and then come to me. If you don't forgive him, I won't forgive you."[26] Sounds like tough love. It is. He is serious. Harboring bitterness and unforgiveness toward others restrains Him from acting on our behalf.

If I come to Him with self-serving prayer out of personal ambition, lust, jealousy, or pettiness, I may be waiting a long time for prayer to be answered, if ever.[27] Wishy-washy prayers are weak. What do they sound like? "I think you are able to help this illness if you want to, but I'm not sure you want to, and if I die, well, I guess that must be what you wanted." Look, as I said, God can answer any cry to Him, and if that is the best you've got, send it up! But there is a better way.

Instead, consider a prayer along these lines: "Father, I know you are willing and able to heal my every sickness, every ailment, every brokenness. By your stripes I am healed! Thank you for healing me and making me whole in the name of Jesus. I give you thanks and praise." Then, consider the matter settled, and live *as if* you were healed.

Some people may say, "Aren't you telling God what to do?" Not at all. I am simply agreeing with what He has told me to do! "By His stripes you were healed," He says in Isaiah 53 and 1 Peter 2:24. My response to this declaration ought to be, "Yes, Lord! I was healed!" Faith is bringing my thoughts and prayers and expectations into alignment with what He has said. This is God telling me what to expect, not the other way around. If He is always willing to heal, to protect and provide, I am coming into agreement with Him. These promises are God-breathed; therefore, they are also God-powered! When we pray in agreement with what God has already said and done, our faith is effective.

Unbelief makes for weak prayers. It is double mindedness: "Maybe He will, and maybe He won't." Some regard such thinking as humble. It is not humility; it is unbelief disguising as modesty. Such thinking turns the sure Word of God into doubt and unbelief. Praying boldly with authority isn't telling God what to do; it is agreeing with Him in that which He has already told us to do! It is trusting Him to honor his promises, his covenants, His Word. "Faith is acting as if God's Word is true."[28]

Our Father is Spirit, and He seeks those who will worship and pray to Him "in spirit and in truth."[29] We must be honest with ourselves and Him in prayer. I know it seems ridiculous to pose or masquerade when talking with God, but I have done it many times. Sometimes, I need to remind myself who He is and to come clean in prayer. No use pretending with Father. And when I face the truth, it empowers me to move beyond any lack or failure.

Silence from Heaven

There are times when the Father seems removed and far away. When this happens, I do two things. First, I do a quick heart check. Psalm 139 tells us to examine ourselves to see if there "be any wicked way in us." If there is something hidden in the corner of our heart, the fix is simple. Confess it to the Lord and ask for forgiveness. Second, I try to recall anyone against whom I am harboring any unforgiveness or if I have crossed someone. If I remember someone, I immediately forgive them and ask God to bless them. If we do not forgive others, God will not forgive us (see Mark 11:26). I need his forgiveness in my life. If I am unforgiving in my life, I find a roadblock I cannot pass in my relationship with Father.

I have learned a lesson about quietness with the Father. Silence does not mean "yes." It does not mean "no." It is just silence. It is a mistake to interpret silence as permission to do whatever we want to do as provision for whatever we have requested. Silence is an opportunity to practice patience. It is also an opportunity to check our own hearts and motives and make sure they line up with His Word.

Once I have checked and cleaned my "side of the street," I begin to praise Him. Psalm 22:3 says, "God inhabits the praises of His people." Praise ushers in His presence. When I turn my attention and affection to Him, my thoughts and problems dissipate, and He inhabits the moment. Soon, I am enraptured and enveloped by His presence, kindness, and love. It is in this secret place with Him that all things become possible.

My to-do list slides to the floor, and I find myself scarcely breathing, not wanting the moment to pass. It is then that the "things of this world grow strangely dim in the light of His glory and grace." These are sacred moments. These are times for which I yearn and ache. His indwelling presence is warm and quickening. The experience is intimate without being overwhelming. I forget altogether the issues of life, basking in His presence and love.

Sin

The trouble with sin, besides killing us, is that it gets in the way of our relationship with Father.[30] It robs us of our confidence to pray. It stands between us and Him.

The key thing about sin is to get rid of it. Quickly. We all fall short. We all miss the target. But we can "be cleansed from all unrighteousness" (see 1 John 1:9). Jesus stands ready to forgive, cleanse, and restore us to right-standing with Father. Sin happens.

We all need to revisit the fountain sometimes. Just be done with it and put it behind you.

Psalm 139 is an invitation for the Father to examine our hearts, to search us inwardly, to see "if there be any wicked way in us." This is a safe place to stand with Him. When we invite Him to examine us, we beat the enemy to the punch. We thwart Satan when we invite correction and receive cleansing by the blood of Jesus.

Patience or Persistence?

Smith Wigglesworth, the "apostle of faith," teaches us to pray for something once and then believe for it to happen. He said, "If you pray for something more than once, the first time is in faith and all the other times are in unbelief."[31] Wigglesworth's rally cry of faith was, "only believe!"[32] To pray once, in faith, was sufficient. Anything more than that is unbelief talking out loud. After all, God isn't hard of hearing, nor does He forget. Once is sufficient.

On the other hand, Jesus taught a parable about the widow repeatedly pressing her case before a hard judge.[33] His lesson was to be persistent in asking. So, perhaps the answer lies in doing both, as necessary. Pray believing the Father hears and answers. But if you don't see the manifestation after a while, pray again.

Prayer of Agreement

There is an especially powerful prayer called the prayer of agreement. In Matthew 18:19, Jesus taught that "if two of you agree as touching anything, it shall be done of my Father who is in heaven." When people ask us to pray for them, we will often have them start and then join them in agreement. According to God's Word, it is done.

Strength in Numbers? Maybe.

I am not so sure about this. I've never felt that I needed to gather a crowd to get Father's attention. The heroes of the faith didn't use prayer chains. They didn't create group texts to get enough people praying to get a breakthrough. The prayer of a single person was enough for Elijah, David, Jesus, and Paul. They obeyed the Word: "If you need help, come boldly to the throne of grace and there you will find the mercy and grace you need."[34] Fervent effectual prayer of a righteous man—one person. Over and over, a single person stood at the pivot point of history, and the outcome changed the world.

On the other hand, there are also examples of power in numbers. Peter was miraculously released from prison because the church prayed for him.[35] Paul asked for churches to pray for him. The Holy Spirit descended on the upper room in a mighty baptism of the Spirit when 120 were gathered together praying.[36]

Perhaps the lesson is, if you have a need, tell Father. If you feel more comfortable with others joining you, do that.

Speak Up

The trigger for a miracle is the spoken word. Bill Johnson teaches that "nothing happens in the Kingdom until something is spoken."[37] Sometimes nothing is happening because nothing is being spoken in faith."[38]

In the realm of God's Kingdom, when we pray the prayer of faith, we acquire the object of our prayer. Answers to prayer occur first in the Kingdom, then on earth. Sometimes, the answers are manifested immediately; sometimes, they aren't. In both cases, it is God who rearranges time, space, and resources to meet our needs. When it takes a while for us to see the answer, it is our responsibility to wait expectantly. As my daughter, Annie, tells her children, "This is a good time to practice our patience."

This is the time in our lives when we wait with faith in our hearts. "Faith is the substance of things hoped for [expected], the evidence of things unseen."[39] Faith is the confident expectation of what has been requested.

In the Kingdom of God, believing is receiving.[40] We have all heard people say, "I'll believe it when I see it!" But the Kingdom of God doesn't work that way. And the truth is, it takes zero faith to live like that. In the realm of the Father, believing is seeing.

What happens when we don't see the answer? Our instructions are to stand believing anyway... until we do. Having done everything, we stand.[41]

The barrier between most people and miracles is unbelief. Most people simply don't believe, trust, or expect God to deliver miracles. I wish I could exempt Christians from that statement, but the fact is that much of the denominational church still teaches that healing, deliverance, miracles, and power were meant for people 2,000 years ago, not for people today. God didn't change. Jesus didn't change. The Holy Spirit, God's power on earth, didn't change. Who changed? We did. God is the same today as He has ever been or ever will be.[42]

ENDNOTES
Chapter Seven

1. "But our God is in heaven; He does whatever He pleases." Psalms 115:3 NKJV
2. Batterson, Mark. "Draw the Circle – The 40 Day Prayer Challenge." (2012). Zondervan. Grand Rapids, MI.
3. "Day unto day utters speech, And night unto night reveals knowledge." Psalms 19:2 NKJV
4. "For as the heavens are higher than the earth, so are My ways higher than your ways, and My thoughts than your thoughts." Isaiah 55:9 NKJV
5. "And when he brings out his own sheep, he goes before them; and the sheep follow him, for they know his voice." John 10:4 NKJV
6. "The Spirit Himself bears witness with our spirit that we are children of God." Romans 8:16 NKJV
7. Federal Bureau of Prisons. "Inmate Statistics." http://BOP.Gov.
8. Johnson, Bill. "Worship – The War of Praise." May 24, 2015. http://www.bethel.tv.
9. "Let us therefore come boldly to the throne of grace, that we may obtain mercy and find grace to help in time of need." Hebrews 4:16 NKJV
10. "Now this is the confidence that we have in Him, that if we ask anything according to His will, He hears us. And if we know that He hears us, whatever we ask, we know that we have the petitions that we have asked of Him." 1 John 5:14–15 NKJV
11. "Therefore I take pleasure in infirmities, in reproaches, in needs, in persecutions, in distresses, for Christ's sake. For when I am weak, then I am strong." 2 Corinthians 12:10 NKJV
12. "And I also say to you that you are Peter, and on this rock I will build My church, and the gates of Hades shall not prevail against it." Matthew 16:18 NKJV
13. "Then he began to curse and swear, saying, 'I do not know the Man!' Immediately a rooster crowed." Matthew 26:74 NKJV
14. Johnson, Bill. "God is Good – He's Better Than you Think." (2018). Destiny Image. Shippensburg, PA.
15. Yeomans, Lilian. "His Healing Power." (2006). Harrison House Publishers. Tulsa, OK.
16. "For I say, through the grace given to me, to everyone who is among you, not to think of himself more highly than he ought to think, but to think soberly, as God has dealt to each one a measure of faith." Romans 12:3 NKJV

17. "So then faith comes by hearing, and hearing by the word of God." Romans 10:17 NKJV
18. "Finally, brethren, whatever things are true, whatever things are noble, whatever things are just, whatever things are pure, whatever things are lovely, whatever things are of good report, if there is any virtue and if there is anything praiseworthy—meditate on these things." Philippians 4:8 NKJV
19. "who through faith subdued kingdoms, worked righteousness, obtained promises, stopped the mouths of lions, quenched the violence of fire, escaped the edge of the sword, out of weakness were made strong, became valiant in battle, turned to flight the armies of the aliens. Women received their dead raised to life again. Others were tortured, not accepting deliverance, that they might obtain a better resurrection. Still others had trial of mockings and scourgings, yes, and of chains and imprisonment. They were stoned, they were sawn in two, were tempted, were slain with the sword. They wandered about in sheepskins and goatskins, being destitute, afflicted, tormented— of whom the world was not worthy. They wandered in deserts and mountains, in dens and caves of the earth." Hebrews 11:33–38 NKJV
20. Cho, David. "God has surely listened and heard my voice in prayer. (Psalms 66:19). http://www.davidcho.com.
21. "'I am the Alpha and the Omega, the Beginning and the End,' says the Lord, 'who is and who was and who is to come, the Almighty.'" Revelation 1:8 NKJV
22. "And if we know that He hears us, whatever we ask, we know that we have the petitions that we have asked of Him." 1 John 5:15 NKJV
23. Tozer, A. W. "Pursuit of God" (2015). CreateSpace Independent Publishing Platform.
24. "And when you pray, do not use vain repetitions as the heathen do. For they think that they will be heard for their many words." Matthew 6:7 NKJV
25. "But if you do not forgive men their trespasses, neither will your Father forgive your trespasses." Matthew 6:15 NKJV
26. "leave your gift there before the altar, and go your way. First be reconciled to your brother, and then come and offer your gift." Matthew 5:24 NKJV
27. "For let not that man suppose that he will receive anything from the Lord; he is a double-minded man, unstable in all his ways." James 1:7–8 NKJV
28. Hagin, Kenneth. "The Believer's Authority." (2009). Faith Life Publications.

29. "God is Spirit, and those who worship Him must worship in spirit and truth." John 4:24 NKJV
30. "For the wages of sin is death, but the gift of God is eternal life in Christ Jesus our Lord." Romans 6:23 NKJV
31. Liardon, Roberts. "Smith Wigglesworth, The Complete Collection of His Life's Teachings" (1997). Albury Publishing.
32. "As soon as Jesus heard the word that was spoken, He said to the ruler of the synagogue, 'Do not be afraid; only believe.'" Mark 5:36 NKJV
33. "Then the Lord said, 'Hear what the unjust judge said.'" Luke 18:6 NKJV
34. "Let us therefore come boldly to the throne of grace, that we may obtain mercy and find grace to help in time of need." Hebrews 4:16 NKJV
35. "Peter was therefore kept in prison, but constant prayer was offered to God for him by the church." Acts 12:5 NKJV
36. "When the Day of Pentecost had fully come, they were all with one accord in one place. And suddenly there came a sound from heaven, as of a rushing mighty wind, and it filled the whole house where they were sitting. Then there appeared to them divided tongues, as of fire, and one sat upon each of them. And they were all filled with the Holy Spirit and began to speak with other tongues as the Spirit gave them utterance." Acts 2:1–4 NKJV
37. Johnson, Bill. "God, He is Better Than You Think" (2018). Destiny Image. Shippensburg, PA.
38. Ibid.
39. "Now faith is the substance of things hoped for, the evidence of things not seen." Hebrews 11:1 NKJV
40. "Therefore I say to you, whatever things you ask when you pray, believe that you receive them, and you will have them." Mark 11:24 NKJV
41. "Therefore take up the whole armor of God, that you may be able to withstand in the evil day, and having done all, to stand." Ephesians 6:13 NKJV
42. "Jesus Christ is the same yesterday, today, and forever." Hebrews 13:8 NKJV

CHAPTER EIGHT

Warfare

The Stakes

There is a battle being waged for our souls.

Our opponent is Satan. He intends to "kill, steal, and destroy" us and our families (see John 10:10). If there is loss, death, or destruction in our lives, it is his doing.

Our savior is Jesus Christ. He comes to bring us life, peace, purpose, and eternal life in the Kingdom of God. If we need healing, provision, grace, love, or compassion, Jesus is our answer. He comes with "healing in his wings."[1] He also brings purpose, hope, peace, and courage.

The Bible is clear: "Whomever you serve is your master."[2] If we choose to follow Satan's voice and his ways, he is our master, and we are his slaves. If we choose to serve Jesus, then He is our Lord. The choice is ours. We vote with our actions, not our intentions. Whichever one we obey is our master, and we are accounted as his followers.

For 38 years, the enemy had his way in my life. Everything I valued was ruined, destroyed. Satan was well on his way to destroying me. But once I was saved, I stepped into Jesus's camp, perfectly equipped to stand against the evil one and to prevail against him. Instead of Satan having authority over me, I have authority over him, in Jesus's name!

The Choice

The choice is clear. God has set before us life and death. He then urges us to "choose life, that it might be well with you and your family!"[3] But, like everything in the Kingdom of God, we have free will; we have the right to choose for ourselves.

Our choices impact more than just ourselves. The men and women we minister to in jails understand this deeply. They get it. The choices they have made have already impacted their husbands, wives, children, and families. When I put the question of life and death plainly before them, almost every person chooses the Lord. They want life for themselves and their kids. They want a future and a hope.[4]

We all need the Lord. We are all bruised, hurt, damaged. We all need healing. We want a future for ourselves and our families rich with goodness, opportunities, peace, and joy. Who wouldn't want their children to live a good life, to be healed and whole, to find meaning and satisfaction? Jesus is the answer to every need and desire of our lives. The other guy brings disease, destruction, and death.

In our lives today, the battle is being waged for our souls. And we get to choose the winner.

The Adversary

God created the angel, Lucifer. Like the archangel, Michael, he was given great beauty and power. But he was jealous of God's glory and became consumed with overthrowing God and "ascending to His throne."[4] Lucifer recruited a third of the angels to his ill-fated quest and set out to dominate the earth. His plot failed, of course, and God banished Him from heaven and denied him access to the throne of grace.[5]

The Jewish people called Lucifer Satan, meaning "adversary."[6] And so he remains until this day. He is responsible for death, wars, famines, diseases, and everything else that serves to kill, steal, and destroy mankind. Satan himself is proof that the nature of evil is the impulse to exert power over others.[7] He is completely obsessed with power, domination, and control. In this quest to kill God's people and destroy the work of God, he shows absolutely no mercy.

Ruler of This World

When Adam decided to believe Satan instead of God, he gave the devil the legal right of dominion over the earth. Adam relinquished the authority God had given him in favor of the enemy. That is why Jesus referred to Satan as the "ruler of this world" in John 12:31 and John 16:11. In the gospel of John, Jesus called Satan "the prince of this world." (John 14:30). Paul echoed the Lord in Ephesians 2:2 saying, "...according to the prince of the power of the air, the spirit who now works in the sons of disobedience."

Satan is the prince or ruler of earth. That is why we endure such calamities, death, and destruction. It is not God causing the mayhem; it is the Adversary. And until he is locked up for a thousand years, he will continue.[8]

Some people ask, "Why doesn't God do something about the devil?" The answer is, "He did." He equipped you and me with weapons to defeat the devil and his minions. He has given us authority and power, in His name, to combat every force of evil in the world. He has armed the church to the teeth. But she is asleep, content, and undisturbed at the moment.

The fact is, God has done everything He is going to do about the devil until after the Tribulation when He will remove Satan from the picture. In the meantime, the Holy Spirit not only restrains the spread of evil, but also, He empowers you and I to combat it everywhere we find it. Let me put it plainly: Sometimes, the enemy runs rampant because we let him.

In the modern era, we have seen this evil demonstrated in the murderous communist regimes of the Soviet Union and China. Marx and Lenin taught the communists that it was communist party's exclusive right to govern and control the people. Only they, the enlightened few, were qualified to govern the ignorant people, because only they were sufficiently compassionate, insightful, intelligent, and enlightened to do so. In the Soviet Union, they murdered more than 20 million of their own people pursuing this philosophy. Chinese communists killed untold millions of their citizens during the Cultural Revolution. Who knows what they would do to Christians in America, given the chance?

Satan is still busy in his quest to control God's creation. He has never stopped pursuing his evil agenda, nor will he until he is destroyed. His agenda and methods have not changed. Today, he is infiltrating the realms of the church, education, government, business, media, arts, and the family. We see the global elites around the world trying to destroy liberty and freedom, the hallmarks of the Kingdom of God and His people. What won't be given to them freely; they will take by force. They will use any means necessary—legitimate or illegitimate—including defamation, lies, and murder. Satan has no mercy. There is nothing that he and his followers will not do to kill and destroy God's people.

The Fight

The battle between good and evil has already been waged and won. Jesus walked out of the grave, descended to Hell, and publicly took back the keys of hell and death from Satan.[9] When Jesus rose from the dead, He won back everything that had been lost because of sin. He then ascended to heaven, returning home to the right hand of God.[10] Jesus won the victory over the enemy.

Satan is not yet stripped of all his power; he still has some. He is at work as an enemy of God. His mission is to kill, steal, and destroy. That's why we still have murders and famines, disease and unrest. He has been stripped of his authority, but his power still remains, for now.

Here's the good news. As children of God, we are under the protection of the Father. We are surrounded, secure, and protected. The blood of Jesus covers us. As Colossians 1:13 puts it: "For he has rescued us from the dominion of darkness and brought us into the kingdom of the Son [Jesus] he loves." Everyone in the world is under his threat, his darkness, except for the children of God. We have been transferred from Satan's domain to Jesus' domain. We are under the protection of the Father. Although we live in the world, we do not belong to the world.[11] We are no longer under the powers and principalities of darkness.

The only way the enemy has access to us is if we give it to him. How do we do that? When we sin, we open ourselves to attack; we become vulnerable. Every time we obey Satan, we open a gateway to ourselves and our family. When we follow him and believe his lies and deceit instead of God, we declare that the enemy is our master. Whenever we decide to align ourselves with the kingdom of darkness, we welcome judgement because that kingdom is judged already (see John 16:11).

Weapons

We are not defenseless against the enemy. We have a protective covering that is impenetrable by the enemy: the blood of Jesus. Every day, I "pray the blood of Jesus" over all my family. As a son of God, I call upon Father to protect and provide for those under my authority, all the ones I love. When I need a quick repulse or attack against him, I fight back by binding the enemy in the name of Jesus and "pleading the blood" of Jesus against him. The Father is attentive to that cry and dispatches the host of heaven to my rescue.

In 1996, the Lord told me that I have spiritual authority over everyone that I love. That doesn't mean I get to stick my nose in their lives and tell them what to do. It means that I have authority to pray for them, to wage spiritual warfare on their behalf. If I love them, I have the legal right to intercede for them before the throne of power. Jesus so loved the world that He has authority for all of us. We have this right and responsibility for all of those we love.

God has given us defensive and offensive weaponry sufficient to win every battle. The "weapons of our warfare"[12] include the sword of the Spirit, which is the Word of God. We also have supernatural armor: helmet, breastplate, and shield. As described in Ephesians:

"Now my beloved ones, I have saved these most important truths for last: Be supernaturally infused with strength through your life-union with the Lord Jesus. Stand victorious with the force of his explosive power flowing in and through you. Put on God's complete set of armor provided for us, so that you will be protected as you fight against the evil strategies of the accuser!

"Your hand-to-hand combat is not with human beings, but with the highest principalities and authorities operating in rebellion under the heavenly realms. For they are a powerful class of demon-gods and evil spirits that hold this dark world in bondage. Because of this, you must wear all the armor that God provides so you're protected as you confront the slanderer, for you are destined for all things and will rise victorious.

"Put on truth as a belt to strengthen you to stand in triumph. Put on holiness as the protective armor that covers your heart. Stand on your feet alert, then you'll always be ready to share the blessings of peace. In every battle, take faith as your wraparound shield, for it is able to extinguish the blazing arrows coming at you from the Evil One!

"Embrace the power of salvation's full deliverance, like a helmet to protect your thoughts from lies. And take the mighty razor-sharp Spirit-sword of the spoken Word of God. Pray passionately in the Spirit, as you constantly intercede with every form of prayer at all times. Pray the blessings of God upon all his believers." Ephesians 6:10–18 TPT

We have power over "all the power of the enemy and nothing shall by any means hurt us."[13] Knowing and speaking the Word of God is our primary offensive weapon. It is called a sword for a reason. Just as Jesus did, we resist the enemy and speak to him what God has spoken to us. When we do, he will flee. One of Satan's tactics is to hide in darkness. Unobserved, he can work his mischief. But when he is discovered, when we call him out, he is vulnerable to our attack and being cast out.

In addition, The Lord gives us power on earth to bind the enemy. "Whatsoever is bound on earth is bound in heaven. And that which we release on earth is released in heaven."[14] So, we bind the spirits of darkness—sickness, depression, suicide, death, and all the others— and release the Spirit of healing, liberty, truth, and so forth, as the particular situation requires. Again, nothing happens until we speak. But when we speak, it is to declare what God says about the situation or to bind the enemy in the name of Jesus.

And then, having done all, we stand. We stand in the great confidence, power, and authority of Jesus.

Testimony

In the original language, the root word for testimony means "to do over, to do again."[15] When I tell others what the Lord has done for me, it releases the power of God to do it again. When I speak to people about Jesus delivering me from addictions, I release the power of God for those people to be delivered too. When we share our stories, we release faith and the Spirit of the Lord do it again, fresh and powerful.

Our testimonies release the power of the Holy Spirit to work. We have seen the effectiveness of testimonies work hundreds of times. Whether we are testifying of healing, provision, deliverance, or peace, the effect is always the same: powerful and immediate. The miracle that God did for us is suddenly available to everyone within earshot of our voices. When we speak to people, the most powerful thing we can do is share our own stories. When we describe what Jesus has done for us, power to "do it again" is released to the person hearing it for themselves.

The power of testimonies applies to everything. When I testify of the Lord's deliverance, people get delivered. When I testify of healing, people get healed. Testimonies unlock faith and power for salvation, peace, provision, and miracles. Truly, the Lord looks for opportunities to "do it again."

When ministering in jails, I often tell my testimony. My life was not so different than many of theirs. And when I tell how the Lord delivered me from alcohol, it releases the power of God to do the same for them. When I tell about the Lord providing jobs and cars and homes and everything I needed to get on my feet, I can feel the faith in the room rise. Every eye is fixed on me, every ear attentive to every word. You can hear a pin drop. And when I tell them that God doesn't play favorites, that what He did for me He will do for them, they lean forward in their chairs, expectantly. Then when I explain the price that Jesus paid, the life available in Him, and that God loves them and has plans and a future for them, the dam begins to burst. Finally, I tell them the choice is theirs: They can choose to continue serving the enemy or choose a new life in Jesus Christ. The choice is theirs!

We have had the privilege of seeing thousands of men and women surrender their lives to the Lord. They call out in repentance, asking Jesus to be their Lord and Savior. And He does.

I have held people in my arms while the Lord miraculously healed them. I have seen demonic deliverances. I have spoken words of knowledge, prophecy and wisdom over people. I have seen visions. But I have never seen a greater miracle than a man or woman repent and give their lives to Jesus under the prompting and power of the Holy Spirit. It is such a special moment of power and joy. Salvation of a man or woman who turns to Him is the greatest miracle of all.

Grace as Power

Over the years, we have confused grace and mercy. Some have defined them as follows: "Mercy is not getting what you deserve, and grace is getting what you don't deserve." The play on words is cute, but the meaning is not always accurate. Mercy is compassion, tenderness, kindness. When God humbles Himself, when He restrains Himself from executing judgement, for example, that is mercy. His mercies are profound and unmerited and fresh every morning.

Grace is different. *Strong's Concordance* defines the Greek term "charis" as "divine influence upon the heart."[16] Webster describes grace as "divine assistance for the sanctification"[17] of believers. In 1996, God spoke to me and said, "Grace is power to do the right thing." The power of grace comes from God. He empowers us to do the right thing.

In 2 Corinthians, the Lord said, "My grace [power] is sufficient for you, for My strength is made perfect in weakness. Therefore, most gladly I will rather boast in my infirmities, that the grace [power] of Christ may rest upon me" (see 2 Corinthians 12:9).

"Let us therefore come boldly to the throne of grace, that we may obtain mercy and find grace (power) to help in time of need" (see Hebrews 4:16).

ENDNOTES
Chapter Eight

1. "But to you who fear My name The Sun of Righteousness shall arise with healing in His wings; and you shall go out and grow fat like stall-fed calves." Malachi 4:2 NKJV
2. "Do you not know that to whom you present yourselves slaves to obey, you are that one's slaves whom you obey, whether of sin leading to death, or of obedience leading to righteousness?" Romans 6:16 NKJV
3. "I call heaven and earth as witnesses today against you, that I have set before you life and death, blessing and cursing; therefore choose life, that both you and your descendants may live." Deuteronomy 30:19 NKJV
4. "'For I know the thoughts that I think toward you,' says the LORD, 'thoughts of peace and not of evil, to give you a future and a hope.'" Jeremiah 29:11 NKJV
5. "How you are fallen from heaven, O Lucifer, son of the morning! How you are cut down to the ground, you who weakened the nations! For you have said in your heart: 'I will ascend into heaven, I will exalt my throne above the stars of God; I will also sit on the mount of the congregation on the farthest sides of the north; I will ascend above the heights of the clouds, I will be like the Most High.'" Isaiah 14:12–14 NKJV
6. Strong, James. *Strong's Concordance.* "Adversary." "Satan." (2010). Thomas Nelson Publishing. Nashville, TN.
7. Burke, L. Morrill. University of Southern Maine. "College Writing." Fall, 1975.
8. "He laid hold of the dragon, that serpent of old, who is the Devil and Satan, and bound him for a thousand years." Revelation 20:2 NKJV
9. "Having disarmed principalities and powers, He made a public spectacle of them, triumphing over them in it." Colossians 2:15 NKJV
10. "So then, after the Lord had spoken to them, He was received up into heaven, and sat down at the right hand of God." Mark 16:19 NKJV
11. "If you were of the world, the world would love its own. Yet because you are not of the world, but I chose you out of the world, therefore the world hates you." John 15:19 NKJV
12. "For the weapons of our warfare are not carnal but mighty in God for pulling down strongholds," 2 Corinthians 10:4 NKJV
13. "Behold, I give you the authority to trample on serpents and scorpions, and over all the power of the enemy, and nothing shall by any means hurt you." Luke 10:19 NKJV

14. "And I will give you the keys of the kingdom of heaven, and whatever you bind on earth will be bound in heaven, and whatever you loose on earth will be loosed in heaven." Matthew 16:19 NKJV
15. Strong, James. *Strong's Concordance.* (2003). Thomas Nelson Publishing. Nashville, TN.
16. Ibid.
17. Merriam Webster Dictionary. (2019). Merriam-Webster Publishing. NY, NY.

Presence

Presence

Many things that occur in the supernatural realm, in the Kingdom of God, are hard to explain with words. They defy description. Our vocabulary is insufficient to describe what is occurring in the supernatural. It is real and unmistakable, and even putting the experience into words lessens it somehow, reduces its nature to something achingly less than the actual experience.

Describing the presence of God can be most difficult. I always feel the Spirit's presence but sometimes more powerfully than others. This is called quickening.[1] I received the baptism of the Holy Ghost in September 1996. Ever since, I have been physically and spiritually aware of the Spirit in me. At that time, I also received the ability to speak in tongues, my private prayer language with God.

Worship and prayer are often key times to experience presence. Often during worship, I have a heightened sense of the Lord's presence in the room. I can "feel" that He is there. The Spirit within me is stronger, more vibrant. He feels like warm oil charged with an electric current. This is simply because the Lord "inhabits the praises of his people."[2] He Himself is present in the room.

Experiencing His presence can be cultivated by focusing on Him, adoring Him, praising Him. When we purposefully turn our attention and focus our affection on Him, we often experience a distinct quickening. My wife experiences Him when she worships Him. Whenever we deliberately seek His face, it seems He is ready to smile upon us.

The Secret Place

Psalm 91 describes a special place called "the secret place of the most high God."[3] It is the place of total surrender to Him. It is a place accessible to every believer in the spirit realm to meet with Father.

It is a place where God breathes His own breath. He meets us in quiet, in holiness, in peace. It is where He "prepares a table for us in the presence of our enemies."[4] In this place, His presence is so great, His peace so profound, and His power so pervasive that our troubles dissipate. They fade away and, frankly, cease to matter, in the power and peace of His presence.

It is this place where we can tell the Father that we are all His, whatever the cost. We abandon worldly affections, all ambition, pride, self. In that moment, we surrender all. We can carry nothing except our own cross. It is that place where we are dead to ourselves and alive to Him. There is no disease here, nor failure, or sorrow, or sadness. There is only Him, radiant and splendid in His fervent love for us. This is the place where all things are possible.

Like the sun peeks over the horizon at the break of dawn, He arises. He shines His face upon us, and we feel the radiance of His brightness and warmth. Alive to Him, He immerses us in His love and glory. We are totally afloat, basking in His buoyant strength.

This "secret" place is available to every son and daughter. Seek His face. Seek His presence. Choose to believe His Word. He will manifest Himself and meet you there.

I have been been saved for 24 years. Through the years, Father has spoken to me many times, and I have enjoyed His presence in my life. However, the most powerful experience of the Lord's presence happened during the time I was writing this book. It occurred without warning, with no special preparation.

A Baptism of Glory

On July 2, 2019, I was praying, and the Lord poured out over me in an unusually powerful way. I am rarely overwhelmed by Him. He is a perfect gentleman and doesn't power over us, beyond what we can handle. But this day was different. He poured out his Spirit, love, and glory so powerfully over me that I was heaving for breath between tears. I was undone.

I was totally immersed in His love, presence, and glory.

To talk about it diminishes the awesomeness of it. Mere words fail. I have no language capable of describing the experience. It was holy and beyond anything I can speak. I felt like Isaiah when he was overwhelmed by the presence of God—"I am a man of unclean lips"—unworthy in the sacred and powerful presence of Him.

I did the only thing I knew to do; I wrote about it:

"Dear Father,

I am undone. I am overwhelmed by your love. I cannot find words to express the depth, width, breadth, and height of your love for me. Words fail me. Emotion pours over me like a waterfall. Every word is swept away by the rushing tide of your passion, knocking me down. Tears wet my face, my tongue is silenced in breathlessness as I await recovery of your comfort and strength.

"Your compassion, patience, love, and kindness for me surpass my ability to tell the story. The enormity of you swallows up the smallness of me. That feeble, fragile, flawed me that dares not raise his face to behold your power and presence. I bow my head and close my mouth in your presence, awestruck and humbled by your glory.

"You are faithful and true in all your ways, Father. You are strength in my weakness, the morning sun in my darkest moments, and my radiant hope for a tomorrow better than today. I am tempted to grieve my failures except that they are missing from me; swept away by your flood of forgiveness: gone, forever. All that remains is you.

"I can scarcely breathe, so heavy is your hand upon me. Relieve me, Father, of your divine presence, that I might breathe and tell the story of your great love and care. Like the sweep of the wind and the torrent of the flood, your power flows over me.

"The more I get to know you, the fewer words I find to describe. Until there is nothing left at all... just to bow the head and fall silent in witness of you.

"Eternity will not suffice to tell of your love for us who call you 'Father.'"

The point of telling this story is that there is so much more to Father than just knowing *about* Him. There is much more to Him than we can know in this lifetime. His sons and daughters will spend eternity discovering more and more about Him and never end.

The fact is, His presence makes me want to stay with Him. My heartfelt satisfaction and fullness for Him is almost more than I can bear. I do not know the full height and breadth and depth of this sweet communion. I bring so little to the relationship; it is just Him holding me.

Peace and power dwell within us. The peace of God saturates our inner selves, driving out our anxiety and fear. Peace transcends and settles the chaos of our minds. And the indwelling Spirit is a constant reminder of Jesus living in us and for us. We are never alone. And never too far from home.

ENDNOTES
Chapter Nine

1. Merriam Webster Dictionary. (2019). Merriam-Webster Publishing. NY, NY.
2. "But thou art holy, O thou that inhabitest the praises of Israel." Psalms 22:3 KJV
3. "He who dwells in the secret place of the Most High Shall abide under the shadow of the Almighty." Psalms 91:1 NKJV
4. "You prepare a table before me in the presence of my enemies; You anoint my head with oil; my cup runs over." Psalms 23:5 NKJV

Epilogue

God created us and called us to be co-creators with Him. He invites us into a relationship with Him that transforms us, our families, our world. He has designed us to be like Him.[1]

Our words have power.[2] They have the power to create and to tear down. They bring blessing or cursing. The words we speak affect others as well as ourselves. What we think and speak alters our brains, our spirits, and our bodies. Our genes are affected by our thoughts and words, which activate or shut down diseases.[3] Our spirits are either quickened or quenched by the meditations of our hearts and the words out of our mouths. For the most part, we have what we say, good or bad. We live in a world of our own creative making.

Jesus said, "My words are spirit and life."[4] So are ours. Life and death are in the power of our tongues[5]. Our words impact the spiritual realm. If they didn't, there would be no point in prayer. We would have no power and authority to bind and loose.[6] Jesus's teachings would be a lie. If we are born again, we operate in the spiritual realm through our spirit. In the realm of the supernatural, in the Kingdom of God, all things are possible.[7] And if all things are possible there, then all things are possible here, in the natural realm. It happens first in the supernatural, then in the natural. God is in charge of the inter-realm dynamic, and it is our privilege to cooperate with Him.

In this way, our words shape our destiny. And not just ours, but also our family's and as many as we love. The Lord taught me years ago that we have authority in the spiritual realm in the lives of everyone we love. That is why Jesus could redeem the whole world, because His love was that great.[8]

Secular people know these principles work for everyone, everywhere. Business leaders and speakers use God's principles all the time to encourage, inspire, and overcome all odds. The children of men are wiser than the children of God. Unbelievers teach the power of ideas and words, the impact of controlling our thought lives and visualizing responses to challenges, physical and mental. They make millions helping people change their lives for the better. The church ignores those very principles. This is why the Church has been weak and powerless for so long. The unbelievers, the business world and secular leaders, have done a better job teaching God's principles than the church has.

The remedy for this powerlessness is to fix our eyes upon Jesus, believe every word He says, and to not give up. And now is the time. The sons of God are emerging in the strength of humility, in the power of love, and the faith of God, and darkness will tremble. This war will be won by serving, not conquering. By loving others, not hating them. By healing, not inflicting wounds. By bringing the power of God to the kingdom of darkness, the sons of God will bring the world an encounter with God, the Good Father.

A generation of church leaders who believe everything Jesus taught is emerging. They are armed with faith, empowered by the Holy Spirit, and ready to assail the gates of hell. They know that His Word is true and meant for us. Today.

All creation eagerly waits to see the arrival of the sons of God.[9]

Endnotes
Epilogue

1. "Beloved, now we are children of God; and it has not yet been revealed what we shall be, but we know that when He is revealed, we shall be like Him, for we shall see Him as He is." 1 John 3:2 NKJV
2. "Death and life are in the power of the tongue, and those who love it will eat its fruit." Proverbs 18:21 NKJV
3. Ellis, Jeffrey. *Forgive*. (2018). Ingram Sparks Publishing.
4. "It is the Spirit who gives life; the flesh profits nothing. The words that I speak to you are spirit, and they are life." John 6:63 NKJV
5. "Death and life are in the power of the tongue, and those who love it will eat its fruit." Proverbs 18:21 NKJV
6. "Assuredly, I say to you, whatever you bind on earth will be bound in heaven, and whatever you loose on earth will be loosed in heaven." Matthew 18:18 NKJV
7. "But Jesus looked at them and said to them, 'With men this is impossible, but with God all things are possible.'" Matthew 19:26 NKJV; "But Jesus looked at them and said, 'With men it is impossible, but not with God; for with God all things are possible.'" Mark 10:27 NKJV
8. "For God so loved the world that He gave His only begotten Son, that whoever believes in Him should not perish but have everlasting life. For God did not send His Son into the world to condemn the world, but that the world through Him might be saved." John 3:16–17 NKJV
9. "For the earnest expectation of the creation eagerly waits for the revealing of the sons of God." Romans 8:19 NKJV

Made in the USA
Lexington, KY
11 December 2019